First published 2002

All rights reserved. No part of this book may be reproduced or transmitted in any form by any means, electronic or mechanical, including photocopying, recording or by any information storage and retrieval system without permission in writing from the author.

Published by POH publishing
Claremont
Castle Gardens
Hay-on-Wye HR3 5DS

Designed by Eric and Tim Pugh

Printed by Europrint U.K. Ltd.
Swindon, Wiltshire.

ISBN: 0-9543918-0-2

© Eric L. Pugh 2002

OLD HAY

IN PICTURES AND PRINTS

*PH*publishing

ACKNOWLEDGEMENTS

To my family for all their help and encouragement. Especially to my daughter, Amanda, who corrected all the grammar and spelling. To Timothy, my son, who spent many hours with me working on the design and checking the historical facts contained in this book, and to my wife June, who tolerated my many hours spent at the computer and helped with all the proofing.

To all the families and friends who donated, or allowed me to scan their precious photographs and prints over the years and for their support during this project.

Brecknock Museum
Margaret Davies
Tony Dean of New Zealand
Edgar Evans
The late Flo Evans
Mary Fairs
Neal Field
Roger Golesworthy
Robert and Mary Golesworthy
The late John Grant
Frank Green
The late R. Trevor Griffiths
Richard 'Dick' Hebbard
Hereford Record Office
Michael Howells
J. Hutchins
Ken Jenkins
The late Rex Jones
Reg and Nesta Lewis
Brynmor Like
Martin Like
Peter and Rita Like
Gloria Madigan

Mac and Nina Maddy
Eric Merriman
Mary Penoyre Morgan
Vera North
Pemberton Books
Barry Price
Dennis Price
The late Percy Price
Julysia Sinclair
Karl Showler
The late Muriel Thomas
Winifred Webb
Adrian Webb
Betty Weir
Sid Wilding
Cherry Williams
Father Richard Williams
Peter Williams
John Williams (solicitor)
Robert Williams
Roderick ('Roddy') Williams
Donovan C. Wilson
The Ordnance Survey Office

CONTENTS

Introduction												VII

Chapter		Page
1	The castles	1
2	St. Mary's Church and the Chapels of Hay	5
3	The bridges	11
4	Castle Street, Castle Square and High Town	15
5	The Pavement, the Town Clock and Broad Street	24
6	Other streets and views	33
7	Buildings, shops and trade	42
8	Events and occasions	50
9	The railway	58
10	The fire brigade	64
11	The schools	67
12	Sports and entertainment	71
13	People, groups and organisations	78
14	The military in and around Hay	85
15	Maps, documents and the old street names	89
	Index	
	List of subscribers	

INTRODUCTION

Hay from The Warren   *photograph by Thomas Moxon 1908*

My family's connections with Hay go back almost 150 years.

Great-grandfather Thomas Pugh was born in Llandeilo Graban in the old Welsh county of Radnorshire. He married Mary Lewis from Aberllynfi in St. Peter's Church, Glasbury, in 1853. Thomas was a skilled shoemaker. They came to live and work in Hay in the August of that year.

I have always had an interest in photography and history. Then, some 35 years ago, our family solicitor, the late and much revered R. Trevor Griffiths, showed me, during a visit to his office, two old photographs of Hay, which I completely failed to recognise. These two full-plate sepia prints were of Castle Square as it was in the late 19th century and can be seen within this book. I was intrigued by their clarity and by the fact that buildings like these had once existed in what is now Castle Square.

I asked Mr. Griffiths if I could borrow them and he agreed. I straightaway went to visit an old friend, John Grant, who I knew was a keen collector of old prints of Hay. He was as interested as I was. Eventually I asked Mr. Griffiths if I could copy them and he kindly gave his consent.

This then started a long co-operative collecting alliance between John and myself. The excitement and discussions that took place when either of us found anything old connected with Hay was marvellous, be it photographs, documents, plans, or prints etc. We even spent hours going through rubbish when we heard that the local District Council was closing in Hay and all required documentation was being transferred to Brecon. Material which was not needed was being thrown out. From this we collected a lot of - to us - valuable records and mementoes. Other friends even rescued items from bonfires during house clearances.

Sadly, John passed away in 1999. However, by then he and I had managed to collect many precious items. The best and most interesting of these are shown within this book.

John and I always talked about publishing a book like this. I therefore dedicate it in memory of John and to the town's most respected historian, the late Geoffrey L. Fairs, who helped and encouraged us so enthusiastically. Most of the historical details in this presentation are taken from his two books, "A History of the Hay" published in 1973 and "Annals of a Parish" published in 1995. Permission to use these has been kindly given by his wife Mary.

I am also grateful to all those people who have given and loaned us old photographs and prints to add to the collection. Their names are acknowledged at the front of this book. Doubtless, older Hay residents will be able to supply and correct names and dates attributed to some of the photographs in this book. My apologies for any mistakes but so many were never supplied with this valuable data, so required in later years, and a certain amount of guesswork has had to be applied.

Eric Lewis Pugh, Hay 2002

Hay from the road to Clyro *dated 1914*

THE PICTURES

For the period prior to the 1830s, prints and drawings, invariably containing a deal of "artist's licence", are our only way of seeing what the locality looked like in the pre-photography years. A few of these appear in this book.

Photography did not appear until the 1830s and certainly not in isolated rural areas such as the Welsh marches until the 1870s. Some of the earlier examples in this book date from this period.

All the photographs, plans and documents have been scanned, digitally corrected and enhanced on my computer system. Many of the originals were in very poor condition, being scratched, faded, torn, and some even partially burned. Where streets and buildings have disappeared, "then and now" photographs are shown which should help identification of the locations. In 1877 the Local Board of Guardians decided to change and update a lot of the street names in Hay. Where possible I have referred to both the old and new names.

I hope this will help to preserve them for future generations to enjoy and to see our little town as it was in years gone by.

THE HAY

Hay is a marcher town, being right on the border between England and Wales, marked by the Dulais brook which flows into the Wye to the east of the town.

Although there was a large camp near Boatside farm on the Radnor bank of the river in the early days of the Roman occupation of Britain, there is no evidence that they ever crossed into Breconshire there, except possibly for occasional forays, and the Roman road from Kenchester to Brecon probably crossed the river at Glasbury and not at Hay. At this time the Welsh occupied the higher ground in the hills, the river valleys being impenetrable jungles.

The known history of Hay begins with the three-pronged Norman invasion of Wales in the 11th century when an attack from Herefordshire was made along the Wye valley in the direction of Brecon by the forces of Bernard de Newmarch, in the course of which Bleddyn, Prince of Brecon, was overcome.

A strong-point was set up at Hay in about 1090 and put in the charge of Sir Philip Walwyn, this being a motte and bailey castle, the mound of which is still to be seen between the cattle market and St. Mary's church. This served to house the garrison until the more permanent stone-built castle was erected in the centre of the town early in the 13th century by Maud de St. Valerie, wife of William de Breos, who had inherited the lordship of the Manor from Milo, Earl of Gloucester.

At this time the town was known by the Norman name of La Haie - the enclosure. Indeed it is still sometimes called "The Hay". The manor was divided into two parts - English Hay, comprising the town, castle and immediate neighbourhood, where English feudal law operated, and Welsh Hay, the much larger area southwards and westwards in the parish of Llanigon and over the Gospel Pass to Capel-y-Ffin. Here the Welsh laws of Hywel Dda were still in force.

The Welsh name for the town is Y Gelli (meaning a grove, or copse) and it is in the county of Powys. This mid-Wales county brings together the three ancient counties of Montgomeryshire, Radnorshire and Brecknock.

THE CASTLES

The building of the first motte and bailey castle took place about 1100 with the coming of the Normans.

An artist's impression of the first Motte and Bailey Castle at La Haia

At this time, of course, there were no roads and many trees. The bridge in the foreground left would have been erected to cross over the gorge containing the Login Brook. Eventually this would have led to the first Norman Church.

"The motte rising 3m to a summit 20m across near the parish church SW of the town is probably the site of the 'castello de haia' which is mentioned in 1121. It was probably built by William Revel, one of Bernard de Newmarch's knights."
From "A Guide to The Hay" 1925.

Hay Castle from a print dated 1830

Later in the 12th century a more commanding site to the north-east was utilised for a large oval ringwork (85 metres by 70 metres). Matilda de Breos is said to have built the stone keep in c.1200, but it is perhaps more likely that she added the gateway arch to a tower built in the 1180s. She died of starvation at the command of King John, who burned the castle and town of Hay in 1216 while attempting to suppress the rebellion of Giles and Reginald de Breos. The town and castle were burned again by Llywelyn Fawr in 1231 and had to be rebuilt by Henry III. In 1232 and 1237 he granted the townsfolk of Hay the right to collect a special toll to pay for walling in the town with stone. The castle was captured by Prince Edward in 1264 and by Simon de Montfort's forces in 1265.

Both town and castle suffered damage by Owain Glyndwr's forces in 1400, but the castle was listed as defensible against the Welsh in 1403. The castle had passed to the Earls of Stafford, later Dukes of Buckingham, and is said to have suffered further damage during the conflicts of the 1460s. The last Duke, executed by Henry VIII in 1521, remodelled the keep.

By the time that the manor house was built in the 17th century, although it was still known as Hay Castle, the original function as a centre of defence and administration had ceased. It now became merely the home of the gentry who played a more or less benevolent role in the town. In 1545 the castle had 'by some irregular means' passed to James Boyle of the House of Grey Friars in Hereford, being granted to him by Henry VIII. Boyle was also Lord of the Manor.

At the turn of the 17th century, Mary, the granddaughter of James Boyle, married Howell Gwynn IV of Trecastle (Trecastell), whose family was to hold Hay throughout the 17th century. It was at about this time that the present mansion was built.

In the early 19th century, the house was occupied by the Wellington family who purchased it from Gwynn family heiresses. The house was restored c.1910, but the eastern part was gutted by fire in 1939. The western part was gutted by a second fire in 1977. This part, however, has been restored and, along with the various outbuildings, is now used for second-hand bookselling.

In 1684 the Duke of Beaufort passed through Hay during a survey of Wales. He was accompanied by a Thomas Dineley who made a series of sketches of the places they visited. This is his impression of Hay Castle with his comments underneath.

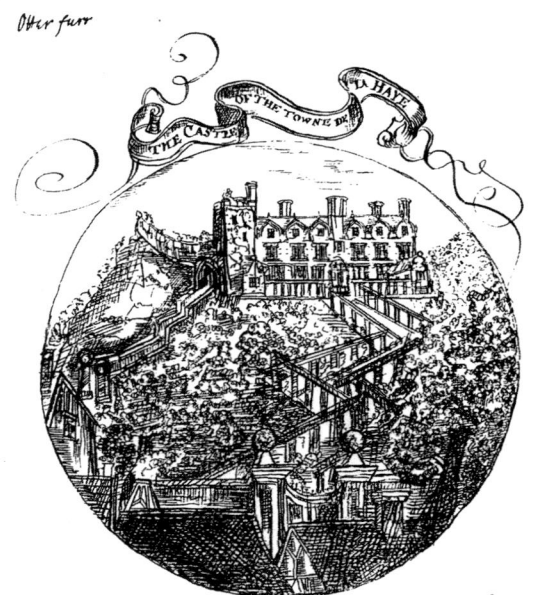

His comments read as follows :
"The Hay As thought by coynes urns and medals there found to have been an ancient plantation of the Romans and since by later ruins it appears to be a place of note.
History sayeth it was once sacked by Owen Glendower.
The vulgar Welsh call the town Y GELHY"

A print of Hay Castle published for S. Ireland dated Mar. 1. 1797

Archdeacon Bevan outside the gate of Hay Castle (c.1875). The Rev. William Latham Bevan came to Hay in 1845 as vicar of Hay St. Mary's Church and remained for 56 years. He lived at Hay Castle during most of this time and became an ardent educationalist in the town, encouraging the establishment of organised schooling. He resigned the living of Hay in 1901 and died in 1908.

See the celebrations of his 50th jubilee at Hay castle, page 50.

The staff at Hay Castle. This photograph was made into a postcard and sent to the boys at the front in France, Christmas 1915.

A view of the southern aspect of Hay castle. The Norman part is on the right whilst the Jacobean Manor part is to the left.
1935

The Castle from the Square. This picture dates from 1930. It is before the War Memorial was moved into a niche built into the wall and is before the fire of 1939. This fire destroyed the eastern part of the Jacobean Mansion.

A different view of Hay Castle taken in 1995 from the top of Hay Clock Tower while the clock was being renovated.

The Castle still dominates the town but is now a second-hand book warehouse and retail outlet.

ST. MARY'S CHURCH AND THE CHAPELS

St. Mary's Church was built on a mound above the river Wye, west of the Login Brook and, as was customary, was sited close to the castle, which was at that time a motte and bailey on the tump. This explains why the church is outside the mediaeval town walls. These walls were not built until about 1237, after the second and larger castle was built *(for details go to 'The Castles' chapter 1).*

The parish of Hay was separated from the pre-Norman parish of Llanigon in the 12th century, at which time the tithes of the Manor of Hay were bequeathed to the new Church of St. Mary by William Revel, Lord of the Manor. The original deed of endowment has disappeared but a transcription of it exists among the Carte Manuscripts in the Bodleian Library at Oxford. It is dated c.1115 - 1120.

The only known print of St. Mary's Church before the complete re-building in 1833. It is from an engraving by Henry Gastineau dated 1830.

In December 1831, Humphrey Allen took the oath before the Bishop's representative on his appointment as first stipendiary curate of Hay. He was a younger son of Sir Henry Allen of Glasbury and great-grandson of Sir Bernard Williams of Gwernyfed - the family who held the patronage of the living.

Humphrey Allen was a man of considerable means and was appalled at the state of the fabric of St. Mary's. He was determined to raise sufficient enthusiasm to have the church, except the tower, rebuilt. The foundation stone was laid after much ceremony in 1833. St. Mary's eventually emerged as it is today.

This photograph is of the toll road leading to Gipsy Castle Lane past the Church. It was constructed in the 18th century to prevent people avoiding the toll gate situated at the bottom of Swan Bank. The side road was to allow people to attend church without paying tolls.

A view of the toll gate c.1880. The Toll Keeper seems quite proud to have her photograph taken. The site of the motte and bailey can clearly be seen behind.

The Guild Chapel of St. John

In addition to the parish church of St. Mary, there is another Anglican foundation in the centre of town known as Church Ifan or St. John's Chapel, which in pre-Elizabethan days served as a chantry for saying masses for particular purposes and also provided a chapel for the Guild of Tradesmen. Little is known, however, of the early history of this church.

Over the years it has been used as a church, a "lock-up", a school, and various shops and commercial establishments. The eastern part was eventually converted back to a chapel in 1934, realigned south and north, and is now used by St. Mary's Church as an alternative place of Anglican worship within the town. The western part of the building is now used as meeting rooms.

No true indications of its appearance before the 19th century have been found. However, some photographs of the building when it had been converted to different commercial premises during the late 19th and early 20th centuries are shown here.

A print from a lantern slide taken by Mrs. Lilwall of Cusop who used to give illustrated lectures around the district during the late 19th century.

This is when St. John's building was a butcher's shop.

The young lady standing in the middle of the right-hand window is Miss E. (Nellie) Lewis who eventually had a butcher's shop of her own in Broad Street.

St. John's Place, looking up towards the Bull Ring. These two photographs were probably taken before the one of Lewis the Butcher, on the previous page, as no name appears over the premises (c.1900).

The Nonconformist Chapels

The Nonconformist Chapels in Hay embraced most of the dissenting churches from the 18th century. The second oldest Baptist Chapel in Wales situated on Bell Bank was founded in 1649 on the site of the existing building. Unfortunately no prints or pictures of the original chapel exist. Most of the other chapels were built in the 19th century and their appearances, from the outside, have little changed.

Some of them are now being used for other purposes than their original religious intent due to the decline in membership and attendances over the last thirty years.

Another view of the Chapel but from St. Mary's Road.

A gathering of the children of the Sunday School outside the old Wesleyan Chapel at the corner of St. Mary's Road and Brecon Road late in the 19th century.

The chapel opened in 1769. John Wesley preached here on 25th August 1774.

By this time (1911) the building had obviously deteriorated considerably. It finally disappeared in the 1970s when it was converted into a house.

This is another photograph derived from a lantern slide by Mrs. Lilwall.

The Pastor, the Rev. William Marwood, at a Harvest Festival in the Congregational Chapel in 1901.

The building stands at the corner of Newport Street and Heol-y-Dwr and has now become the 'Globe Gallery'.

The Congregational Sunday School at a tea at Cooper's Hall, Cusop, in 1911.

(Author's mother fourth from left, second row from front.)

The Baptist Sunday School on this photograph taken in the Cae Mawr Meadow in 1912.

Mr. Ralph Jones (tailor and outfitter) was presented with a radio for his forty years as organist at the Baptist Chapel. Mr. Herbert Stephens from the " Tower Café ", an elder of the Chapel, made the presentation in February 1963.

THE BRIDGES

This is one of the oldest photographs taken in and around Hay. It shows the remaining part of the original stone bridge built in 1763 which was swept away by a flood in 1795. The wooden "temporary" structures lasted until 1863 when Thomas Savin built the new cast iron bridge during the construction of the steam railway at Hay. This photograph obviously pre dates the Savin designed structure.

The elegant cast iron bridge built by Thomas Savin in 1863. He was the contractor to the Hereford, Hay & Brecon Railway Company who converted the old Hay to Brecon Tramroad to carry the "modern" steam locomotives. The bridge lasted until 1957 when it was replaced by the existing bridge.

Both these photographs were taken at the turn of the 20th century.

Owing to confusion over the granting of the collection of tolls on the original bridge over the river Wye in 1763, local people were led to believe that the lease on these tolls would cease after 98 years. Consequently, on 1st October 1861, 300 people from Hay and Clyro approached the toll gates amid great celebrations, only to be refused free passage by the toll keeper. The angry crowd tore down the gates, threw them into the river and put the toll keeper in fear of his life. The riot lasted for two days, only coming to an end when the authorities were able to convince the people that the Bridge Commissioners had, by act of Parliament, authority to continue with the tolls in order to maintain and keep the bridge in good repair.

The need for tolls continued for many years and they were not withdrawn until the 31st March 1933.

These pictures show the crowd gathered for the occasion and the first horse-drawn vehicle to cross Hay Bridge without paying tolls. In the cart are Mrs. Jones from Upper Lloyney, Clyro, and Miss Hannah Probert of Cefn-y-Betws, Clyro.

The gates come down at last.

Mr. Reg Pugh from Llowes (in the cap) assists in the process.

Between 1955 and 1957 a new bridge was built across the Wye. It was opened with due pomp and circumstance on 14th January 1958.

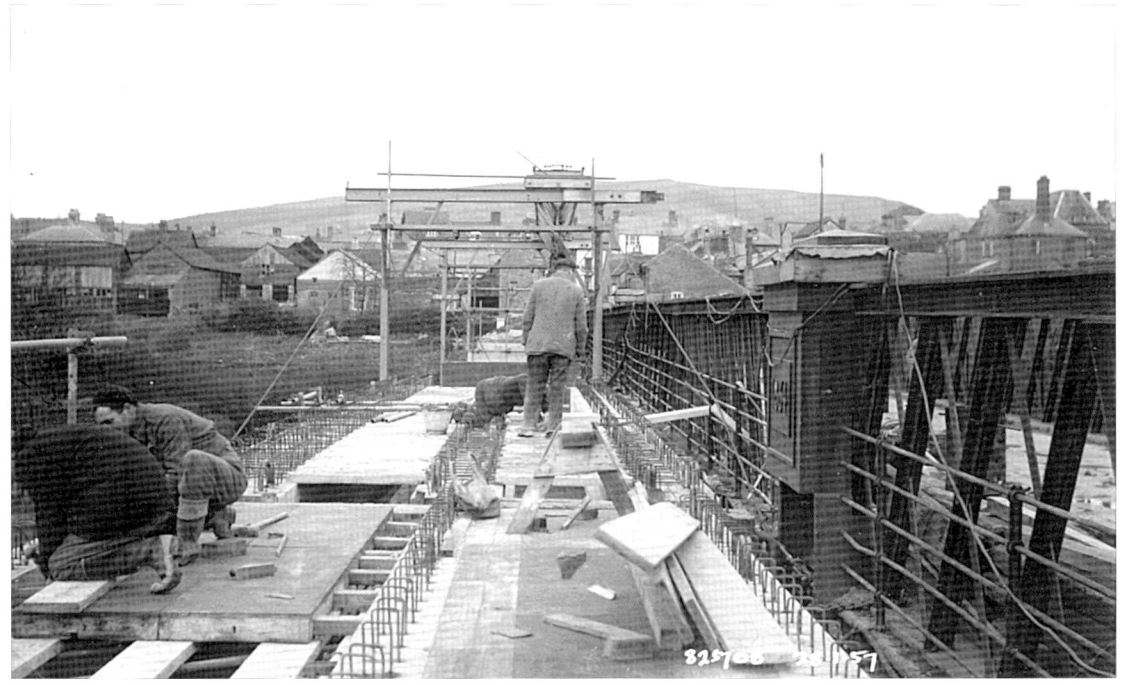

Some of the many photographs which were taken during the building period. These are dated January 1957.

The new structure was placed to the east of the old iron bridge built by Savin in 1863.

Photographs of the opening of the new bridge on 14th January 1958, performed by County Alderman Garnet Morris (on left) and County Alderman G. R. Davies (centre), accompanied by the Chairman of the County Council, a multitude of schoolchildren and people from the town and district.

CASTLE STREET, CASTLE SQUARE AND HIGH TOWN

This is one of the oldest photographs taken in Hay (c.1870). The cottages on the left-hand side must have been demolished some years later (pre-1890). This is Castle Street as Kilvert would have known it. (*Shown on frontispiece.*)

Mr. Horden outside his shop in Castle Street (later Grant's). The Rev. Francis Kilvert was a frequent visitor to this shop, which also ran a savings bank to which Kilvert subscribed.

A view of the shops at the top, western end of Castle Street. The cottage in the 1870 photograph on the previous page has disappeared and this smart new shop has appeared. No details have been found about Tucker's but this photograph must have been taken before Thomas Moxon (see below) took over the premises in 1890. He then altered the shop front again.

One of Hay's most memorable shops - Moxon's of Castle Street.

Thomas Moxon was a renowned photographer and businessman. This advert appeared in the 1908 edition of the Town Guide. The shop closed in the early 1950s. *See a photograph of the wedding of Thos. Moxon on page 79.*

Again looking towards High Town and Castle Square. The old Talbot Inn can be seen on the left (c.1930).

Castle Street in 1949.

The same view in 1955.

Looking east towards Castle Square. Moxon's Emporium is on the immediate left. *Dated 1914*

Madigan's Cycle shop which, for almost 45 years from 1920, was situated at the top end of Castle Street. This also became the booking office for the Plaza cinema. A photograph from 1920 shows a chauffeur and his immaculate motor car outside the premises.

22, Castle Street, which is the shop front on the right in the photograph above, when it was occupied by T. Williams, butcher, c.1930. The premises are now occupied by a shop selling fancy goods and souvenirs.

This photograph, taken a little further along Castle Street in 1922, shows a wall where a shop named 'Enigma' is now situated. The little boy is Michael Stapleton, who was killed during the Second World War, and the lady is believed to be Mrs. Joan Like, when she was Miss Joan Davies.

The Blue Boar c.1910. On the left-hand side can be seen the gap and part of the wall which is shown in the photograph above.

A photograph taken from the Blue Boar of a parade making its way towards the Town Clock, looking down Church Street towards the Swan Hotel, c.1900.

Castle Square

High Town before 1870 when the buildings on the right occupied what is now Castle Square. This was one of the photographs that Mr. R. Trevor Griffiths showed me thirty years ago.

Just the peak of the still-existing Cheese Market can be seen in the top middle distance.

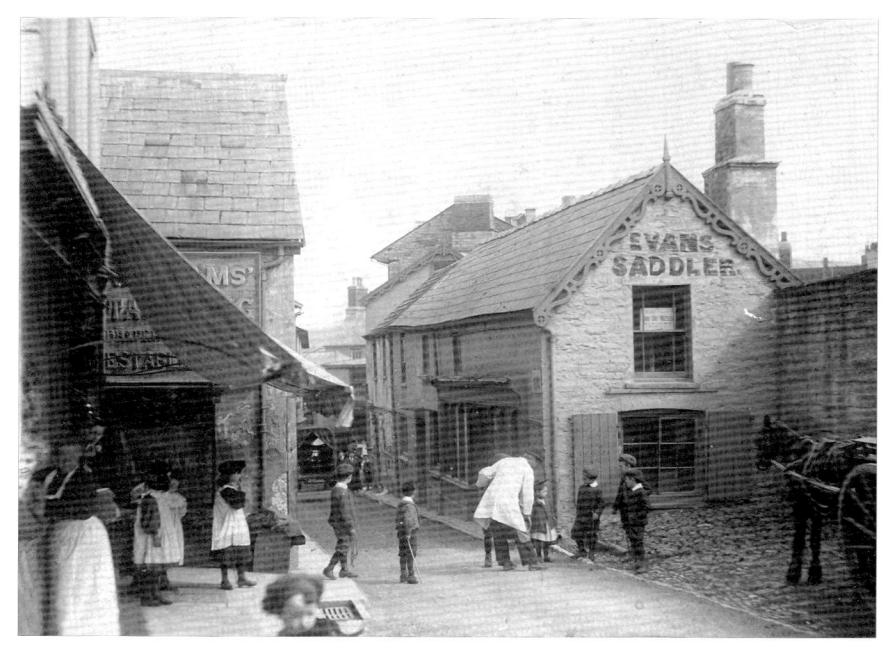

The same view now, 2002. All the shops in the middle of the photograph above were demolished in the 1870s.

To see a contemporary plan of the demolished buildings, go to the 'Maps and documents' chapter.

A view of the same buildings as above but from the rear aspect and a later photograph. The buildings are here in process of being demolished. The low building to the left of the one with the extended eaves was known as "The Corn Market". The gateway shown extreme right is still there at the side of what is now the HSBC Bank building. This gateway led to what was then "The Fountain Inn".

Castle Square in 1932. The War Memorial is still in its original position and Thomas Stokoe's soft drinks bottling works and offices stands where the HSBC bank is now.

A photograph taken during the 1930s when the bottling works was being demolished to make way for the Midland Bank (now HSBC).

A Remembrance Day parade passes Castle Square in 1952. The Bon Marché and the Market Tavern, which can be seen on the right-hand side, were both demolished in 1954.

High Town

Two pictures of High Town derived from lantern slides taken by Mrs. Lilwall of Llydiartywaun, Cusop. c.1885

The top one shows a scene looking up towards Castle Street.

Where the HSBC Bank now stands, can be seen the soft drinks bottling works.

Davies, the chemist, is on the right-hand side. This is where Armstrong purchased his "dandelion poison" in the early 1920s. *For details of Herbert Rowse Armstrong see page 80, chapter 13.*

Looking across High Town towards Giles, the ironmonger. This must have been a Thursday, Market Day. *c.1885*

Shops at the east end of High Town c.1900.

A few years later, about 1925, and cars have appeared.

THE PAVEMENT - BROAD STREET - THE TOWN CLOCK

The Pavement, which was known as Cranbourne Alley until 1877.

The centre left of this photograph from c.1890 shows Cater's drapers and milliners shop. This was, and still is, known as Cranbourne House. The name is derived from The Pavement's original name of Cranbourne Alley. A second large display window was added to the right-hand side early in the 20th century.

No. 2, The Pavement, c.1890.
See also the photograph on the right.

William (Bill) Pugh (1901-1995) outside No. 2, The Pavement in 1960.

He sold sweets, tobacco and "made-on-the-premises" ice cream. Bill and Doris (author's parents) had the shop from 1934 to 1974.

The Town Clock from The Pavement on a market day in 1930.

The Pavement is decorated to celebrate the investiture of the Prince of Wales in 1969.

Snow blocks The Pavement in January 1982.

A modern fire appliance is used to repaint the Town Clock in 1984.

A print from 1814 of the area known then as "The Tump". This view looks up "Cranbourne Alley" (now The Pavement) with the King's Head on the right-hand side. Golesworthy's shop now stands where the barn is situated on the left-hand side.

Hay Town Clock was built in 1884 at a cost of £600 on "The Tump".

1911 at the Town Clock, when the people of Hay in County Huron, Canada, presented a flag to the people of Hay, Brecknockshire.

The Rose and Crown in Broad Street. This was demolished in 1875 and subsequently became the Crown Hotel. It closed as a hotel at the end of the 1980s and was turned into flats.

The part of the building on the extreme right-hand side with the bay window became the present Rose and Crown Inn. The Seven Stars is the building above the double gates. This photograph must have been taken about 1870.

Towards the end of the 19th century, when the annual May Fair was held in Broad Street. This early photograph was taken from the window of what is now the council offices. In those days it was the vicarage for St. Mary's Church.

A meeting of the members of Hay Free Church United organisation at the Clock in 1912.

A large gathering at the Town Clock c.1890 of the Ancient Order of Foresters. There appear to be three different chapters attending.

The Town Clock being renovated and painted in 1928 at a cost of £45. The contractors were W. Lewis & Son of Hay.

Note the wooden scaffolding.

Charles Terrett's grocery shop which is now F. W. Golesworthy's lower shop. Charles Terrett was obviously a prominent citizen of Hay. Through details on other photographs of the period he was a member of the fire brigade, the Hay Volunteers (army), the Foresters and other worthy organisations.

In 1900 one of the largest trees on the Moor Estate was felled and brought down through town, past the Town Clock, to be cut up at Robert Williams' timber yard. This set of photographs shows the scene of the felling and its transportation down through town.

The Town Clock c.1912. The difference to be noted is the appearance of a post box outside where the council offices are now situated. Also there is no gateway in the wall to what was then the vicarage for St. Mary's Church occupied by the vicar, Rev. J. J. De Winton.

Market day by the Clock in 1920.

Market day c.1930.

The western end of Broad Street just by the Town Clock. The building next to what is now Tinto House was demolished in 1890. The new building then became a doctor's surgery and is now a book shop.

1912

Kedwards, grocer in Broad Street. Now David Williams, butcher.

1920. Cheese and Armstrong, *(see page 80)* solicitors, occupied the offices on the right-hand side.

Market day in 1920.

A photograph dated 1901.

Looking east on a Market day in 1900.

OTHER STREETS AND VIEWS AROUND HAY

Oxford Road which, before 1877, had been called Horsefair Road. In this photograph taken about 1890 it is still being used as its original name depicted.

Swan Bank at the turn of the 20th century. At the turn onto Brecon Road there were railings guarding the brook. It was so quiet that chickens could safely use the road.

A view from the tower of St. Mary's Church in 1885. The noticeable difference is the large barn situated in the orchard where Hay Cinema Bookshop now stands.

"Chain Alley" in Newport Street. These were originally almshouses and were often visited by Rev. Kilvert. They were demolished about 1880.

The same view as above but taken in 1969. The area on the left was known locally as "Cats Park". It now contains a small estate of modern bungalows.

Although not really in Hay but just a mile from town, the Moor at Hardwick in 1868. The first house was built on the site in 1550 by James Penoyre and was extended and altered in 1825-1828. The front and side were added to the original house and can be seen on this photograph. The house was requisitioned and occupied by the US army in World War II and demolished in 1951.

The bottom end of "Pig Lane", so-called because the town's pig market was held there before 1850. It is now called Chancery Lane. The 16th century buildings were demolished just after this picture was taken in 1965. The original print was on 8mm cine film and this photo has been digitally reproduced from one frame. The site now contains the new library building.

Photograph taken during the demolition of the houses in Chancery Lane in 1965.

Oxford Road looking east, c.1885.

The building on the right-hand side, which was demolished in the 1970s, used to be a coaching stables and ticket office. In the opening through the middle there was a ticket lobby set into the wall.

The Swan Well. Although little changed now, the undergrowth and height of the trees have made it less open.

In Brecon Road, these cottages were demolished in the 1960s to make way for the new fire station and a new dwelling house. It was called Oak Row. The only building remaining is the house on the immediate left, now called Golden Oak House.

The shop in Brecon Road when it was two cottages in 1890.

A photograph of Hay from the Warren by Thomas Moxon, c.1900. Note the hedge running down through the middle.

Market Street at the turn of the 20th century. The weekly china market is being held outside what is now the Royal British Legion Club. The little house - since demolished - tucked into the corner by the Butter Market can be seen. The area occupied by this house was minute and is now part of the pavement area on the eastern side of Market Street.

An early photograph taken in the new cemetery which the Board of Guardians developed in Brecon Road. This became a necessity when the churchyard at St. Mary's Church became full in 1877. The photograph here is from this period as there are no gravestones.

The sundial is still at Hay Cemetery but has been moved in recent years to improve access.

In 1884 Sir Joseph Bailey laid out the river walk now known as the Bailey Walk at his own expense and gave it to the town. In 1897 to commemorate Queen Victoria's Jubilee the walk was extended from the river bridge to Wyeford Road.

These three views show the Bailey Walk as it was between 1900 and 1920.

Two views of the Mill at Cusop. The one on the left was obviously taken several years before the lower one, as the house on the right-hand side had not been built.

Dates are uncertain but both are from the latter half of the 19th century.

A view of the Cae Mawr and castle orchard, taken from Hay Castle. The orchard is now the town car park. Photograph c.1925.

The railway running around Cusop Hill to the brickworks. Remains of the works can still be seen at the top of Cusop dingle.

Two more photographs by Thomas Moxon taken in the late 19th century. These are taken by the 'Steeple Pool" looking west towards the railway station on the far right bank.

Looking across the cast iron bridge down Bridge Street in 1950. This bridge and the toll house on the right were demolished in 1955 to make way for the new bridge.

An aerial view of Hay taken by Donovan C. Wilson of Hereford in 1950. The cast iron bridge built by Savin in 1863 can still be seen, together with the railway station complex. There are also virtually no television aerials.

BUILDINGS, SHOPS AND TRADE

Buildings and houses in and around the town which have now been demolished or have had their appearance very much altered over the years.

The Three Tuns in Broad Street. This photograph was taken while the building was being renovated in 1975. The building is an early 17th century timber framed building incorporating part of a 16th century three bay cruck truss structure. Next to the Castle it is probably the oldest building in town.

A photograph from the late 19th century taken on market day looking down Bridge Street towards the bridge. The Three Tuns can be seen on the right-hand side with the Black Swan opposite.
Shown on frontispiece.

Frank Cadman's, seed and feed merchant in Broad Street, c.1912. These shops are now an office and private dwelling.

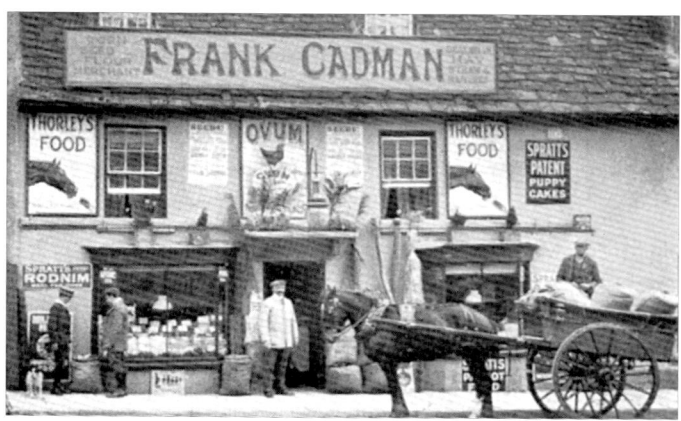

The old Ship Inn, situated at the top of Newport Street then known as Ship Pitch. The last landlord was William Williams (author's grandfather). It was demolished for road widening in 1978.

This photograph c.1911.

Another view of the old Ship Inn, just before demolition. This is the view looking up Ship Pitch (Newport Street) from the east.

The Black Lion Inn in Lion Street, c.1910.

The building, although little changed externally since this photograph, has been extensively altered internally. It is now the Old Black Lion Hotel.

The cottages known as "The Salt Box" in Oxford Road. They were where the precious commodity of salt was kept in the 18th and 19th centuries. These were demolished c.1910. The entrance lane to the Cae Mawr meadows is on the extreme right-hand side.

The first post office in Hay c.1895. The proud postmaster is showing off his family and staff. The original telegraph office pole can be seen to the left of the building. The building is now called Radnor House and is situated at the junction of Oxford Road and Church Street.

An advertising drawing from the middle of the 19th century.

This etching hung in the manager's office at Robert Williams & Sons Ltd. for over a hundred years. It is dated 1865.

Another advertising drawing, here for Giles, the Ironmongers, in High Town.

In front of Robert Williams & Sons Ltd. ("The Limited"), 1910. The only known person is Herbert Williams, second from right, who went on to become General Manager.

The Half Moon in Lion Street, c.1930. This public house became "dry" in the 1960s and was turned into flats.

From a photograph of 1910, Gwilliams of Paris House. The front of the shop was completely remodelled in the 1920s.

Gwilliams ceased trading in the 1980s. It is now the Red Cross Shop.

H. G. Williams, butcher in Lion Street, (opposite the Black Lion) in 1923. The shop now sells antiques.

Another prominent business family name in Hay during the 19th and 20th centuries was Webb. The founder of the firm was a James Webb who arrived in Hay during the 1870s to work as a stonemason in the town. Within a few years he had set up a carriage building and undertaking business in an old building situated in Church Street on the later J. V. Like's site. The photograph opposite is of the interior of this workshop and shows James Webb standing on the right surveying men who are believed to be his two sons, Humphrey and Frank, at work. This old print dates from the later years of the 19th century.

James Webb's company expanded and was eventually taken over by his two sons. They then built a new workshop in Lion Street. This was situated where the Bethel Chapel now stands, opposite the Drill Hall. The photographs below are scenes of both inside and outside these premises. The degree to which the firm expanded can be seen by the display of the hearses drawn up outside. Most of these photographs come from the 1890s.

They also opened a retail shop at 3, Lion Street (now Davies, newsagents). The shop seemingly specialised in the sale and repair of cycles. Mr. H. V. Webb is stood on the left.

J. L. Davies and Son, chemists, at 7, High Town in 1910. Oswald Martin, the solicitor concerned in the infamous Armstrong murder case, married the daughter of the owner.

H. W. Gwatkin, the cash grocer, in Lion Street. It eventually became Evans' Stores and is now a Chinese 'takeaway'.

An advertising calendar for Gwatkin can be seen in the 'Maps and documents' chapter.

The opening of Maddy's new bakery on Bell Bank in 1910.

George Pitt is on the left with his son, William, on the right-hand side. The gentleman in the middle is unknown.

Laying new gas mains in Church Street in 1935.

Amongst the group are Bert Breeze, Ted Maund and members of the Gibbons families.

Thomas Pugh, fishmonger and fruiterer, in Lion Street, 1927. Left to right in the photograph: Thomas Pugh, Tony Pugh, Dorothy Pugh (née Baker), Hilda Parry (née Pugh) and William (Bill) Pugh (author's father).

Two views of Robert Williams and Sons ('The Limited') timber yard, Hereford Road, taken in 1968 just a few years before it closed.

The site is now occupied by a builders' merchants.

World War II. Bryne's shop and café in Bear Street with some visiting British soldiers and Mrs. Bryne.

EVENTS AND OCCASIONS

Some memorable occasions which have occurred in Hay over the years.

The jubilee of Archdeacon Bevan, Vicar of Hay, at Hay Castle in 1895, celebrating his 50 years as vicar of the parish, here shown with his family.

When the diarist Rev. Kilvert was a curate at Clyro, he was a frequent visitor to the Castle and the Bevan family.

Archdeacon Bevan and his wife Louisa had three daughters, Alice, Frances, and Ellen, and a son, Edward, who became the first Bishop of Swansea and Brecon.

A photograph of Bishop Bevan appears in the 'People, groups and organisations' chapter.

Castle Street decorated for the Coronation of George V in 1911.

The Civic Sunday parade descends Church Street in 1911.

Church Sunday School pupils parade in 1914.

This group photograph shows members of Hay Male Voice choir after giving a concert at Hay Castle in 1911. The only known are: top row, second from left, Herbert Williams of "The Limited", middle row, second from left, Tom Pugh (later fishmonger and fruiterer), and bottom row, fifth from left, Donald Maddy (grocer).

1890, and a new row of houses is being built on the Cusop road. They became Albion House and Albion Terrace.

1925. The staff of H. V. Webb pose for a photograph outside their works in Lion Street. By now they had moved from their old premises to the opposite side of the road. These premises are now occupied by Philip Gittins.

The unveiling of Hay War Memorial in Castle Square in 1920, to the fallen of the First World War. The memorial was later moved back into a recess in the Castle wall, when the names of the fallen in the Second World War were added. This series of photographs was taken on the occasion of the original 1920 dedication.

The annual 'Hay Horse Show' was, until the 1950s, held on the show field at Brecon Road. This photograph shows the exhibition stand for H.V. & F.W. Webb at the show in 1900.

In 1913 a flying exhibition visited Hereford, and Tom Stokoe, a member of a prominent Hay business family (the soft drinks factory in Castle Square and the Crown Hotel), became one of the first men in Hay to fly in an aeroplane. This is a souvenir presented to him after his experience.

In 1930 severe rainstorms flooded Brecon Road and caused the cancellation of the annual Hay Horse Show.

In 1925 the then vicar of Hay, Rev. J. J. De Winton, had acquired a model 'T' Ford. In order that he could transport all his friends and relations he had H. V. Webb and Sons make a trailer to pull behind the car. The vicar took this photograph of his wife at the wheel and a full "load".

The builders at the completion of the new Conservative Club in Lion Street, 1930.
Left to right: F. Smith, Rhys Harding, E. Price, H. Webb, unknown, J. Webb, R. Smith, Tom Neale, unknown, Bill Lewis, Percy Layton.
Seated: C. Jones, unknown, and J. Slater.

The floods in March 1963 when the river Wye pushed back the Dulais Brook and caused the scenes depicted here at Dulais Terrace, the gas works and the surrounding area.

The Town Gas Works had most of its area under water. Much of the machinery and all the retorts had to be replaced.

Hay and Cusop Women's Institute.
A meeting of the just formed institute, complete with some in fancy dress, at the Parish Hall, c.1947.

The manually operated telephone exchange closes in Hay in 1966.

The last team of operators at the exchange which was located in the building facing the Town Clock on The Pavement. This is now a restaurant.

Left to right: June Pugh, Gladys Turner (supervisor), Jennifer Williams and Valerie Morgans.

THE RAILWAYS

Hay had one of the earliest railways (horse-drawn tramway) in the country. The Hay Railway opened from the Brecknock and Abergavenny Canal at Brecon to Hay on 7th May 1816. The line was opened from Hay to Clifford Castle on 30th July 1817. The line was not completed between The Lakes at Clifford and Eardisley until 1st December 1818 because of the problem of the river crossing at Whitney.

An old print of Hay dated about 1830. It shows the old tramway (horse-drawn) in operation. Reproduced by kind permission of Brecon Museum and Art Gallery.

A stone lithograph dated 1830. It shows Hay and the tramroad from the northern bank of the river Wye.

The Hay Railway was sold to the Hereford, Hay and Brecon Railway which made use of parts of its route in 1860. The H.H. & B. was a struggling local line, much of it built by Thomas Savin, contractor and builder of many Welsh lines. It was completed in 1864.

Looking west towards the bridge over the river, 1920.

Like most local lines it was eventually rescued by a larger company; not the Great Western, in whose territory it might be thought to lie, but the Midland, which used it and other lines which it acquired or had running powers over, to put together a through route from Birmingham to Swansea via Hereford, Brecon, the Neath and Brecon Railway and the Swansea Vale Railway.

The Midland began working the H. H. & B. in 1869, leased it in 1874 and absorbed it in 1885. The Midland's metals ended five and a half miles west of Hay at Three Cocks Junction where they joined the Mid-Wales Railway.

The "down" train from Brecon, c.1880.

The train to Brecon being pulled by an 0-6-0 under Hay bridge, c.1920.

The "up" train to Brecon passing under Hay Bridge, c.1910.

The Golden Valley Railway, which had its northern junction at Hay and ran through the Golden Valley to Pontrilas, was built between 1876 and 1889, was closed down in 1898 and then rescued by the G.W.R. in 1901.

It survived as a passenger line until 1941 and goods until the 1950s.

Looking east towards Hereford, 1948.

Looking towards the town from the "down" platform, 1955.

Inside Hay signal box, 1960.

Photograph taken from River Wye Bridge, 1930.

The "down" train from Brecon and the "up" train from Hereford. Both photographs taken in the late 1950s from the station footbridge.

Sadly, the whole of the Hereford to Brecon lines including Hay were completely dismantled in 1963 under Dr. Beeching's infamous axing of most of Britain's branch lines. These photographs are of the dismantling at Hay.

THE FIRE BRIGADE

The first reference to a fire engine in Hay is in 1843. In 1849 the Vestry issued a scale of charges for the services of the fire engine shown here. This sheet was found amongst rubbish saved in 1974.

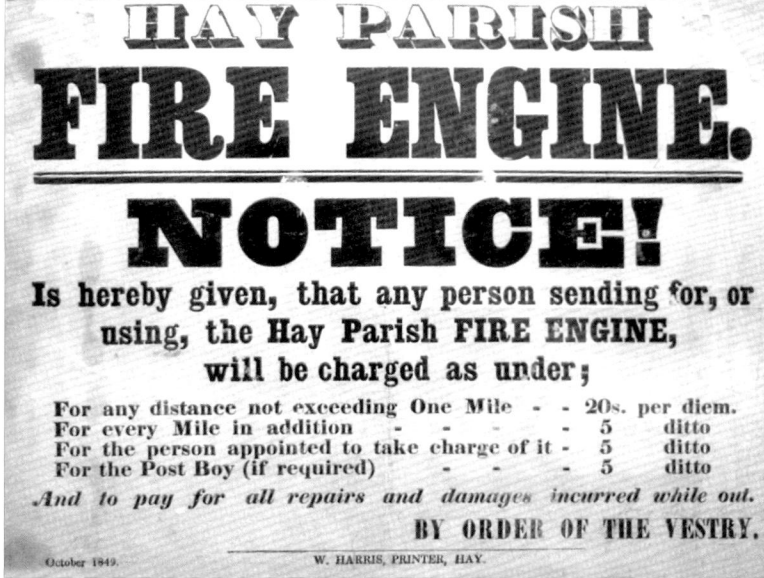

The fire engine figured frequently in the minutes of the Local Board of Guardians from 1865, mainly relating to the purchase of galvanised buckets and hoses etc. The original engine was a hand-operated pump manufactured by Merryweather and purchased in about 1840. On 4th May 1893 the Board "considered it advisable that a fire brigade be formed and that Mr. C. T. Evans be asked to take command and procure the names of 10 suitable men and another officer to form the brigade". This photograph shows the brigade giving a demonstration at The Warren in 1895.

Uniforms of the period 1900 to 1940 are shown here. Lieutenant William (Billy) Williams on the left and Fireman William (Bill) Pugh (author's father) in 1928, on the right.

Nothing more relating to the brigade was recorded until the Urban District Council minutes in 1901 discussed the purchase of a new steam engine. This photograph from 1902 shows the brigade proudly showing their new steam engine, which became locally nicknamed "The Firefly", outside the newly built (in 1901) fire station on Bell Bank.

Captain C. T. Evans is seen standing on the right with his lieutenant and firemen.

Horses were used to pull the engine until 1925 when a secondhand farm tractor was purchased. Many tales of derring-do and hilarity arose from this period.

Also taken outside the fire station on Bell Bank. This time the men are in their brass helmets and the horses are harnessed.

These horses were kept in a field on the Radnor side of Hay Bridge. Apparently they were extremely difficult to catch when they saw a uniform!

A photograph from 1926 taken in Oxford Road. Left to right: Capt. Edgar Evans (son of C.T. Evans), Lt. Billy Williams, Fireman Bill Pugh is without his hat in the centre and Firemen Eric Evans and Wilfred (Blower) Turner on right-hand side The remainder are all from the Lewis, Webb and Price families.

Hay Fire Brigade on display in 1911.

Back row, left to right: Harry Lofts, Bob Williams of The Seven Stars, Edgar Evans, Jim "Tip" Evans, Fred Southgate.

Front row, left to right: "Breezer" Webb, Lt. Charles Terrett, Capt. C. T. Evans, Frank Webb of The Mason's Arms.

"The Firefly" steam engine was finally sold to a garage in Whitney for pumping water at the beginning of World War II and was eventually scrapped for the war effort.

Hay N.F.S. in 1941 outside the fire station in Church Street (now a bookshop).
L to R: Eric Evans, Wilfred Turner, Lt. Billy Williams, Geoff Jones, Alan Price, Jack Vaughan, Alan Davies, Tony Birch, Percy Price, Bill Pugh, Rex Evans, Tom Lewis, Roy Lewis, Jeff Price, Tom Evans and Captain Edgar Evans seated.

THE SCHOOLS

After the closure of many of the small private schools throughout the town, in 1825 the National Society of the Church of England founded a church school in Hay for boys and girls. This was erected in Brecon Road in 1827. It became known locally as the "National" or "Church" school.

This is one of the earliest photographs taken of the Church school. The title underneath reads: "Mrs. Barrett and Mr. A. G. Barrett (Headmaster). June 7th 1877".

Mr. Barrett was headmaster from 1864 until 1891. A portrait of him can be seen on page 80, chapter 13.

The Church School with staff and pupils on 1st July 1904. By this time Mr. Harry Morris had become headmaster.

He, too, appears in the chapter on 'People, groups and organisations'. He served at the school from 1891 until 1927. His wife taught the infant classes.

Empire Day in 1912 when the Dowager Lady Glanusk hoisted a flag in the school playground which had been presented to the school by children from Hay, New South Wales.

The Church/National School held their infant classes at the Parish Hall in Lion Street. This group shows the staff and pupils in the playground in 1895.

The 'British' school movement was started in England and Wales in order to provide schools in which the religious instruction was non-denominational. When the "Goff"* free school in Hay was closed on Bell Bank, a new school was built in Heol-y-Dwr in 1877.
*See Geoffrey L. Fairs, 'A History of The Hay'.

Pupils and staff outside the school in 1910 (author's mother ninth from left, middle row).

Staff and pupils in 1916. The building was demolished for the new police station to be built in 1967.

1930. The only pupils known to author are Lucy Powell now of the Three Tuns (second from left, middle row) and Doreen Williams, later Mrs. Gerald Morris (fourth from left, middle row).

The staff including Mr. Jones (on left), headmaster, and pupils at the British or Council school in Heol-y-Dwr in 1939.

Pupils and teacher from the British (Council) school on a nature walk in July 1948.

Left to right, standing: Mike Williams, John Meredith, Donat Price, Bobby Woods, Peter Hall, Graham Bowen, Maureen Davies, Clarice Price, Jack Lewis, Rita Lloyd, Wendy Like, Bryn Morris, Tony Crook, John Williams, June Williams, Marion Joseph, Greta Webb.

Front row: Rob Smith, Luther Jones, Bernard Pritchard, Eric Pugh, David Jones, Rosemary Simmonds, Gillian Lewis, Jean Prosser and Joyce Simister. The teacher Mr. Prosser is standing at rear of the group.

SPORTS AND ENTERTAINMENT

Archery was introduced by the Bevan family when they lived at Hay Castle. In spite of this, the diarist Kilvert disapproved of the proposal to form an archery club in the town in 1872; in his diary for 15th March he says: "I don't consider it desirable or practicable." One wonders why, when so many of his friends - including the Morell and Llanthomas families - were keen toxophilites.

This photograph was taken in the Castle orchard. It is now part of Hay Primary School complex. The building in the middle distance is still there.

Hay hockey team in 1905.

Standing: Pugh Morgan, Jack Herd, unknown, unknown.
Second row: J. Edwards, A. J. De Winton, Garnet Williams.
Front row: W. Ramage, C. Hinks, E. Mayall, R. T. Griffiths, unknown.

In 1921 the then vicar of Hay, Rev. J. J. De Winton, who was a keen football enthusiast, decided to form a team from the church choirboys. He called them Hay St. Mary's F.C. and the name has been used ever since.

These are the members of that 1921-22 team outside Hay Parish Hall. The members are as follows: back row, left to right: Laddie Vale, Jack Cartwright, Eric Hitchcox, Herbert Batts, Eric Evans and Herbert Harris. Front row, left to right: Vanie Crompton, Stuart Batts, Tom Lewis, Ashby Webb and Hugh Mortimer.

The Golden Valley Hunt meets at Hay Castle in 1920.

Names or when and where this photograph was taken are unknown. The only indication available is written on the back of the print, "Hay Cycling Club".

Dressed up for a game of cards in 1911. Left to right: Billy Williams, Walter Shepherd (The Drill Hall), Rupert Maddy and Edgar Evans.

Hay St. Mary's football team in 1925. The only names known are:

Back row, left to right: Eric Evans, Herbert Harris, unknown. Front row: unknown, unknown, Trevor Batts, Frank Pritchard. Extreme right, Sidney Hyatt. The remainder are unknown.

Hay St. Mary's F.C. in 1923.

In the 1920s "The Hay Players" was formed by Rhys Harding, the choirmaster for St. Mary's Church. The society performed several Gilbert and Sullivan comic operas. This group is from November 1924 at Hay Drill Hall in 'The Mikado', where they performed for four nights, with matinées, to full and enthusiastic audiences.

Tennis at the old Liberal Club in 1933.

L to r: Betty Williams, Ruth Hitchcox, Len Sayce, Joyce Williams and Stewart Batts.

1934 and Hay St. Mary's F.C.'s win over Hereford United football club on their own ground at Edgar Street in the Hereford Cup.

A golf club was founded about 1912, originally on the Warren and later, when this was found to be inadequate, on Hay Common near the reservoirs, where a sporting nine-hole course was laid out. This photograph was taken at the opening ceremony in c.1930. Many local people are here, including the Grant and Madigan families who were prominent in the establishment of the club.

Hay St. Mary's Football Club 1933-34
T. Lewis, A. James, S. Evans, H. Lewis, A. Birch, W. Vick.
J. E. Rees, P. Evans, D. Price, P. George, W. Gundy, F. Wells, T. Batts,
E. Powell, P. E. Hughes, D. J. Pugh
A. Jones, I. Massey, T. Price, I. Morgan, T. Pugh, S. Batts, S. Bowen, G. Lewis

Hay St. Mary's 1951.
Left to right - back row: Bernard Jones, Geoff Turner, Laurie Price, Ernst Guller (the Crown Hotel), Sid Lowrie, Reg Probert, unknown, unknown, Cliff Carr, Trevor Price, Ernie Griffiths.
Front row: unknown, unknown, "Oakie" Jenkins, Albert Powell, Ishy Jones, George Powell, unknown.

At the Coronation carnival in 1953. The initial gathering of the parade always commenced on the green outside Hay railway station and proceeded up through town to the show field in Brecon Road.

A carnival in 1970. Hay Women's Institute posing for a photograph outside the "Tanner's Arms" in Broad Street.

Rear: Mrs. Eddie Williams, Mrs. Prosser, Mrs. Irene Webb, Mrs. Mary Davies, Mrs. Havard.
Front: Mrs. Rosie Wright, Mrs. Blake, Mrs. Blackmore, Mrs. Jones, Mrs. Bamfield, Mrs. Symonds, Mrs. Price ('The Star'), Mrs. 'Tabby' Price.

PEOPLE, GROUPS AND ORGANISATIONS

John Percival Jones, who was born at Nantyglasdwr, Cusop, in January 1829. He was taken to the USA as an infant where he grew up to become one of the richest men in America. He was Senator for the state of Nevada.

John Games in his capacity as town crier, outside the gates to Hay Castle. He was born in Hay in 1812. His father, also John Games, was clerk at the Hay, Hereford and Brecon tramroad weighbridge office in 1816, which building is now Warren Cottage. The younger John then became a barber in the town and his shop was in Cranbourne Alley (the Pavement). He lost his wife and three children between 1841 and 1851 according to census returns.

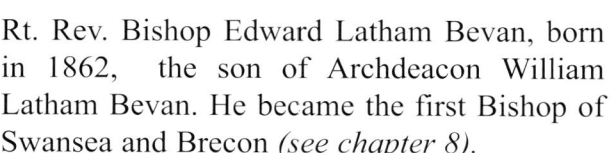

Rt. Rev. Bishop Edward Latham Bevan, born in 1862, the son of Archdeacon William Latham Bevan. He became the first Bishop of Swansea and Brecon *(see chapter 8)*.

The wedding of Thomas Moxon who took many of the original photographs shown in this book. He married Sarah Ellen Owens (Nellie) on Wednesday 30th September 1903. Mr. Ernest Mayall, jeweller and watchmaker of High Town, Hay, was best man. This photograph was taken in Oxford Road.

Some local lads at their 'retreat' on the river bank opposite the Warren in 1909. Why it was called "Spike Island" no-one seems to know. Left to right on this photograph are Tom Pugh (fishmonger), Bill Pugh (carpenter), unknown, Billy Williams (the Ship), Tom Thomas (the Blue Boar) and Fred Watkins (baker).

Alan G. Barrett who was the headmaster at the Church (National) School in Brecon Road from 1864 to 1891. He was born in Gloucestershire in 1844. His wife Mary assisted him at the school.

The much-revered Harry Morris, headmaster at the Church School from 1891 to 1927. His wife taught the junior classes which were held at the Parish Hall. They lost their only son, Lt. Charles Geoffrey Morris, on the Somme in October 1916. The small Chapel on the left-hand side in Hay Church was donated by them, in memory of their son.

Herbert Rowse Armstrong.

Armstrong was one of the most celebrated murderers of the twentieth century. He was the only solicitor to be hanged in Great Britain. He came to Hay in 1906 to become the partner in a firm of solicitors in Broad Street. Armstrong and his wife lived at Cusop. He was accused of poisoning her with arsenic and after a sensational trial in 1922 was found guilty and hanged at Gloucester jail. The case attracted international attention.

For full stories of the case read "Exhumation of a murder" by Robin Odell, published by Harrap in 1975 and "Dead not buried" by Martin Beales, published by Robert Hale Ltd. in 1995.

Any photographs relating to the Armstrong case are heavily copyrighted and unable to be reproduced here.

Hay Board of Guardians outside 'The Union' (Cockroft House) in 1929. The board consisted of such people as Major Cockroft, Rev. J. J. De Winton, Dr. Thos. Hincks and the Hon. Mabel Bailey.

Members of the St. John's Ambulance Brigade on parade at the Town Clock in 1947.

Left to right: Mrs. W. Wilson, Miss Ellen Jay, Miss Bebb, Mrs. Frank Golesworthy, Miss Beryl Jones, Miss Thomas and Miss Vaughan.

Doctor and Mrs. W. Wilson in their roles as officers in the Hay branch of St. John's Ambulance Brigade. Dr. Wilson was a popular 'G.P.' in Hay for many years. His surgery and home were at Tinto House in Broad Street.

The Church Lads' Brigade outside the Parish Hall in Lion Street in 1910.

Rhys Harding, organist at St. Mary's Church and organiser of local musical productions during the 1920s and 1930s, including many of the Gilbert & Sullivan comic operas.

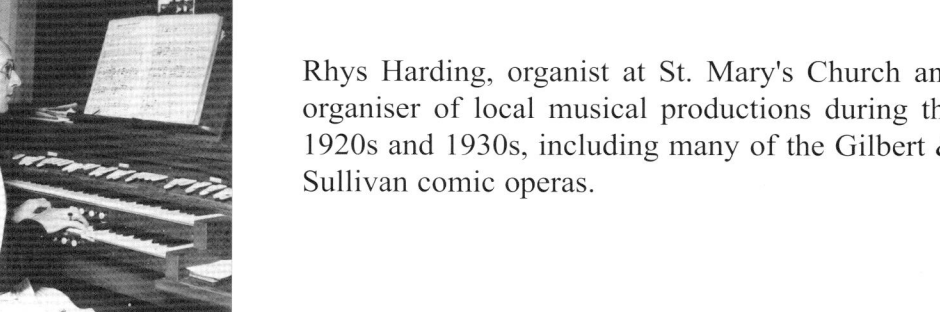

The Church Lads' Brigade in 1928.

Back Row - L to R: W. Gundy, A. Jones, F. Gammond, H. Sedgewick, W. Mayall.
2nd Row - L to R: J. Jones, H. Webb, R. Lewis, J. Jones, W. Cotterell.
3rd Row - L to R: G. Maund, J. Lewis, H. Harris, R. Harding, L. Vale, C. Rosser, V. Leighton.
4th Row - L to R: W. Keylock, R. Keylock, R. Knight, J. Evans, G. Davies.
Front Row - L to R: J. Gibbons, R. Hartwell, G. Keylock, D. Turner, L. Jones, P. Evans.

The Royal Antediluvian Order of Buffaloes meet at the Crown Hotel in 1950.

Hay Urban District Council in 1960 at the Town Clock. Left to right: Arthur Golesworthy, Donald Maddy, Albert Breeze, Ernest Mayall, James James, Dorothy Birch, Thomas Pritchard and E. Tarrant (clerk).

Mr. Herbert "Bumper" Howells, town crier in Hay from 1935 until 1982, here outside the Cheese Market in Castle Square, when he had been provided with a new town crier outfit complete with tricorn hat. Mr. Howells became the longest serving town crier in Hay.

The inauguration of Ken Smith as the new town crier on 25th October 1985. Also present are the then Chairman of Hay Council (on left) Mr. Ken Ratcliffe, and Mr. John Williams, the steward for the Lord of the Manor, who invested Ken with his warrant and bell.

THE MILITARY IN AND AROUND HAY

Hay ("D") Company, 1st V.B. South Wales Borderers.
Winners of prize for 'Smartest and best drilled company',
Aldershot 1892.

The band section of the Hay Volunteer Battalion parading outside the Drill Hall c.1895.

Another photograph of the Volunteers but this time taken in Hay. This possibly shows the Hay company. Lieut. Griffiths is the officer and Charles Terrett is standing on the extreme right. Many of these faces appear in the fire brigade photographs of the time.

For many years during the 19th century the Royal Horse Artillery used the land surrounding Hay Bluff as a training ground. Their camp was usually situated near to New Forest farm. In September 1877 the renowned photographer Bustin of Hereford was asked to take a portfolio of photographs for the Daily Sketch in London. These photographs subsequently appeared as etchings in this national newspaper.

This series of photographs courtesy The Bustin Collection, Hereford Record Office.

This photograph and the following ones on the next page were recently discovered in Hereford. They show soldiers from the Victorian age as they really were.

Cusop Hill can be seen in the background of this picture.

A gun cleaning session.

The field kitchen.

This view, taken from the road leading to Hay Bluff, shows the camp in the field opposite the farm buildings, which can just be seen towards the lower left.

The weather apparently, for the whole week during Bustin's visit, was appalling. It is remarkable he was able to obtain such good prints in those conditions using the cameras which were available at the time.

The regimental blacksmiths at work.

The Hay Territorials in Aden in 1928.

A photograph taken during the early part of World War II of the Hay and Talgarth company of the Home Guard. Several faces are familiar to the author. They are: first left, middle row, T. D. Nutt, the chemist; fifth from left, middle row, Henry Moses, who taught carpentry at Hay Council School; eighth from left, middle row, Jim Yule; first left, front row, Bernard Jones who became captain of the local army cadet force; and fourth from left, front row, Spencer Hall, owner of the Central Garage in Broad Street.

MAPS AND DOCUMENTS

An account of a dreadful storm which occurred in Hay on 25th September 1585. The only original copy still in existence is in the Newberry Library in Chicago, USA. This is the frontispiece of the leaflet.

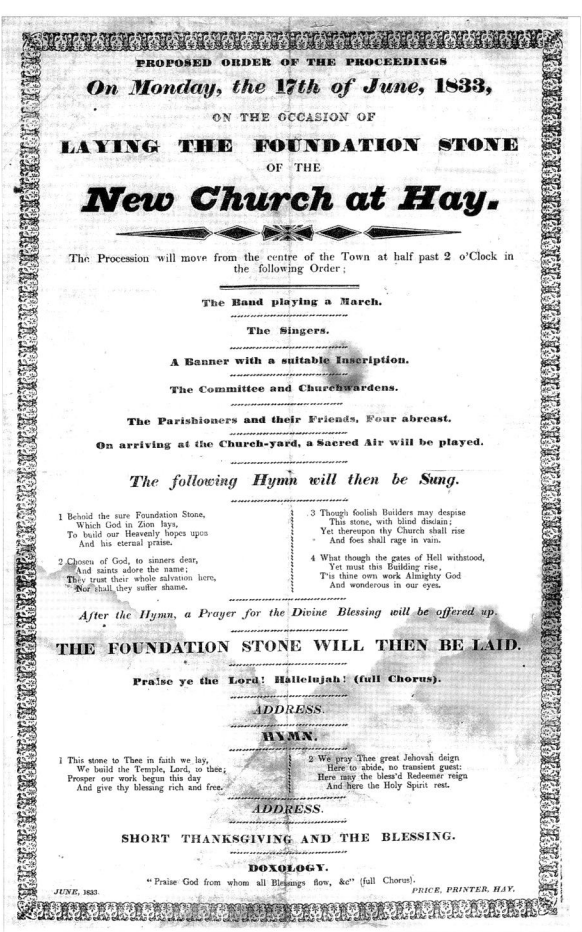

A copy of the poster advertising the ceremony of laying the foundation stone for the "new" St. Mary's Church at Hay on Monday 17th June 1833.

It states that "A procession will move from the centre of Town at half past 2 o'clock in the following order - The Band playing a March - A Banner with a suitable Inscription - The Committee and Churchwardens - The Parishioners and their Friends, Four abreast - On arriving at the Churchyard, a Sacred Air will be played".

The poster was printed by Price, printer of Hay.

The original poster is still at St. Mary's Church.

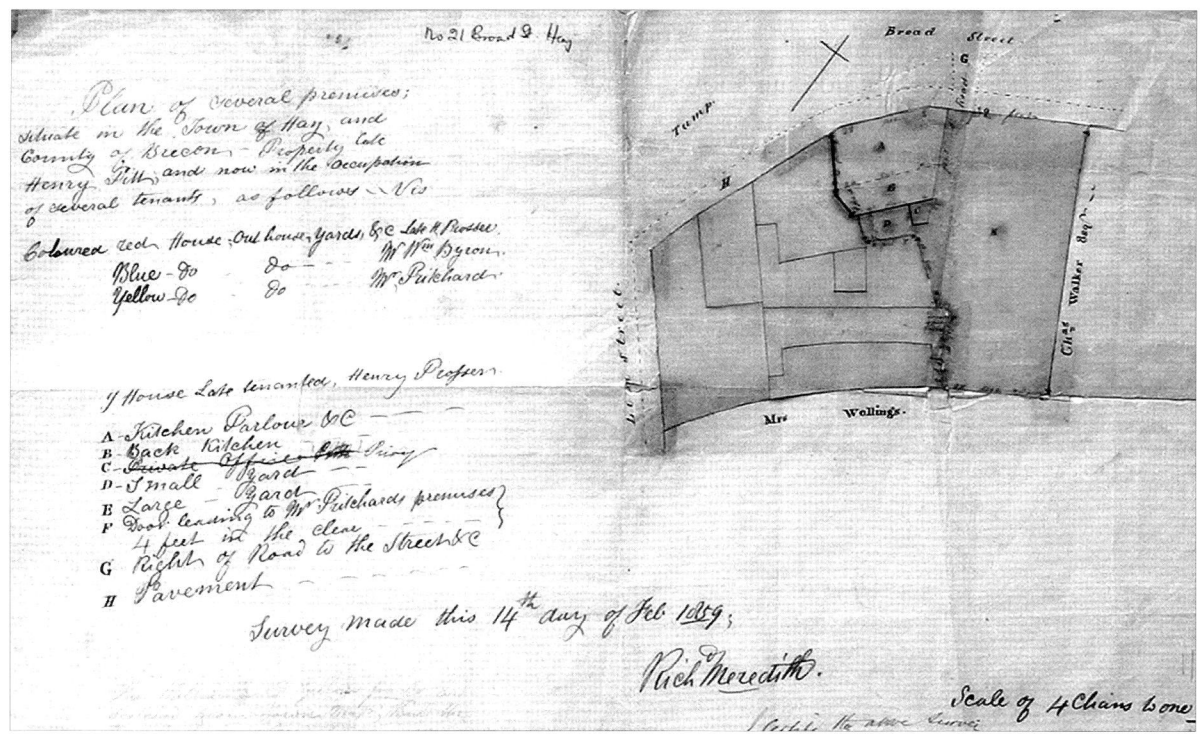

A survey plan of the corner of Lion Street and Broad Street, where Golesworthy's shop now stands. The plan is dated 14th August 1859 and must have been drawn to show who owned which premises in the area. The Town Clock had, of course, not been built at this time and the area where it now stands was called "The Tump" (see print "At The Hay" in chapter 5).

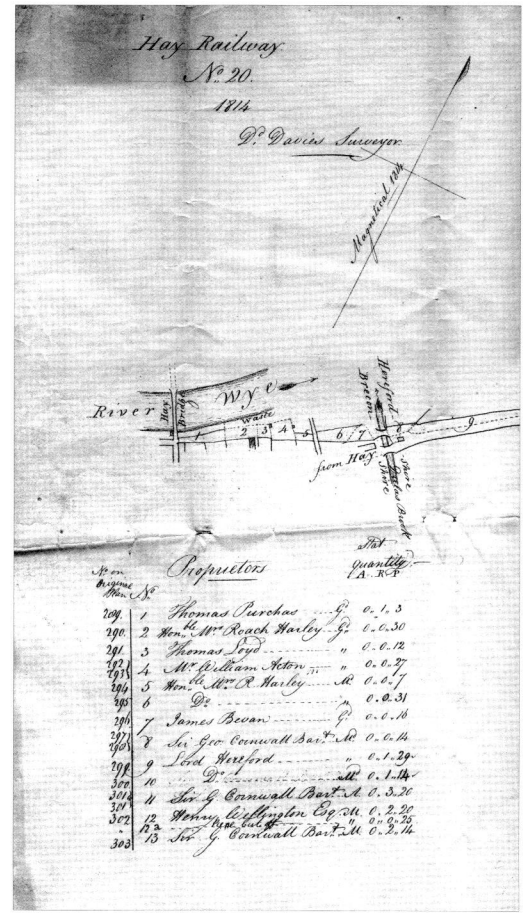

Part section of a large map drawn by D. Davies, surveyor, in 1814 to show who owned the land around the area at the eastern end of town. This was in order that the owners of the Hay, Hereford and Brecon Tramway could negotiate with these landowners for the purchase of the ground required for the tramway terminus at Hay.

The areas are set out in acres, rods and poles and show the names of the individual owners.

This area, in 1863, became the site for Hay railway station.

A street plan, this time showing the layout of the buildings then occupying what is now Castle Square. Unfortunately, there is no date shown on the plan. The properties on the right-hand side of the drawing show the outlines of the buildings which were eventually demolished in 1870-75. A photograph of these buildings can be seen in chapter 4 under the heading Castle Square. The Market Tavern, demolished in 1954, can be seen opposite the 'Town Hall' which we now know as the Cheese Market.

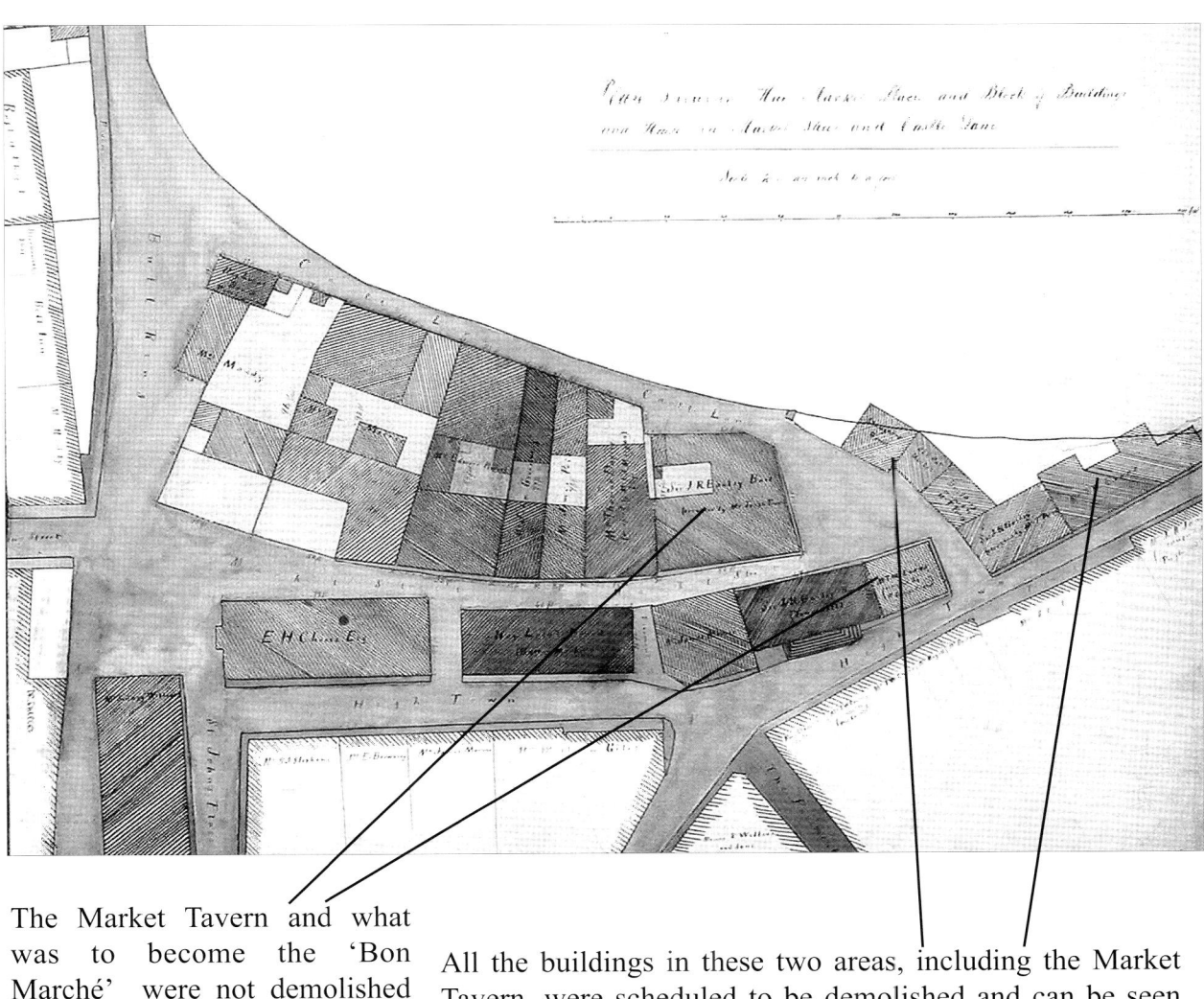

The Market Tavern and what was to become the 'Bon Marché' were not demolished until 1954.
(See page 21, chapter 4.)

All the buildings in these two areas, including the Market Tavern, were scheduled to be demolished and can be seen during this process on page 20, chapter 4.

These plans were probably drawn up because the Board of Guardians proposed the building of a new large, Victorian-style market hall in the present Castle Square. On the next page the plans and elevation drawing of this proposed hall are shown. The proposals obviously never transpired.

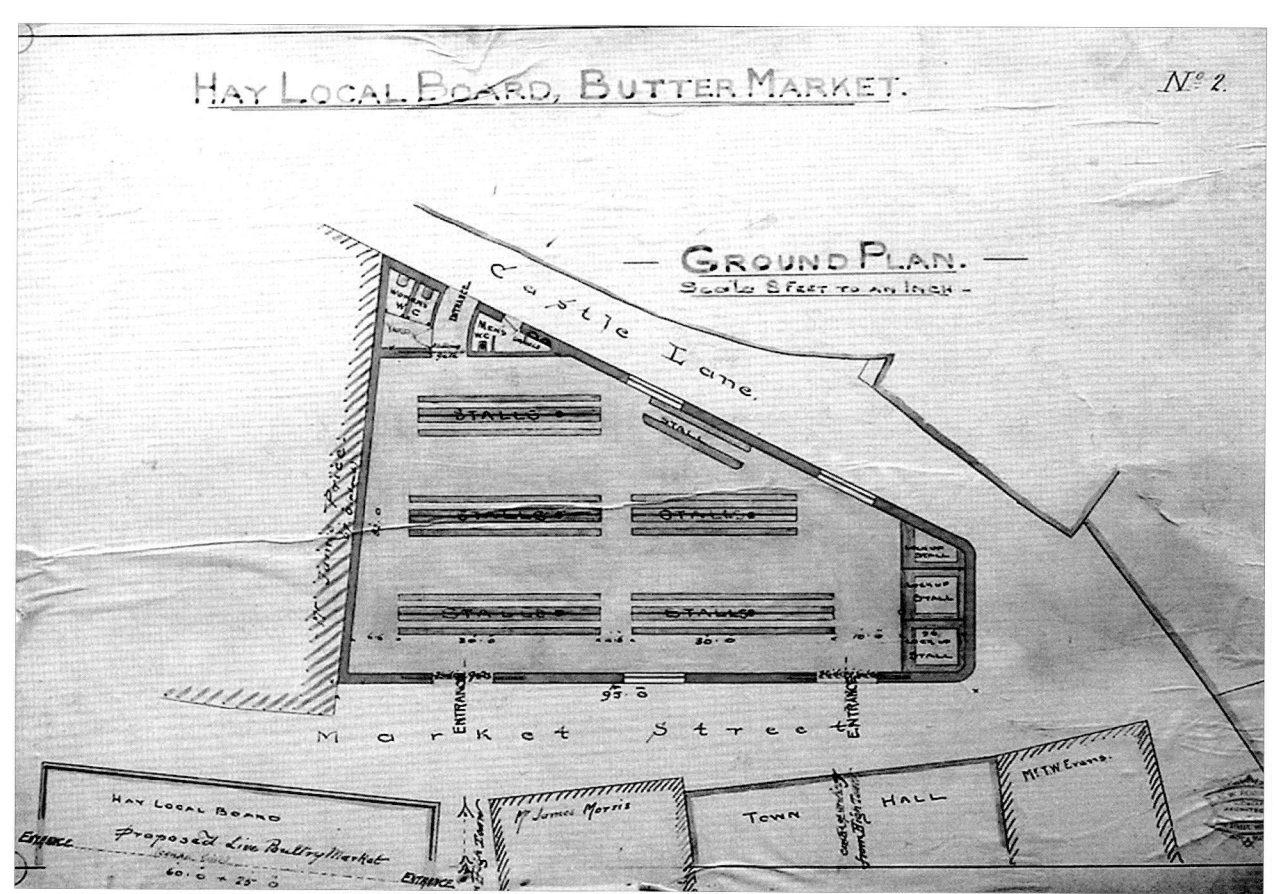

This plan shows the area the new market hall would have occupied - virtually the whole of Castle Square.

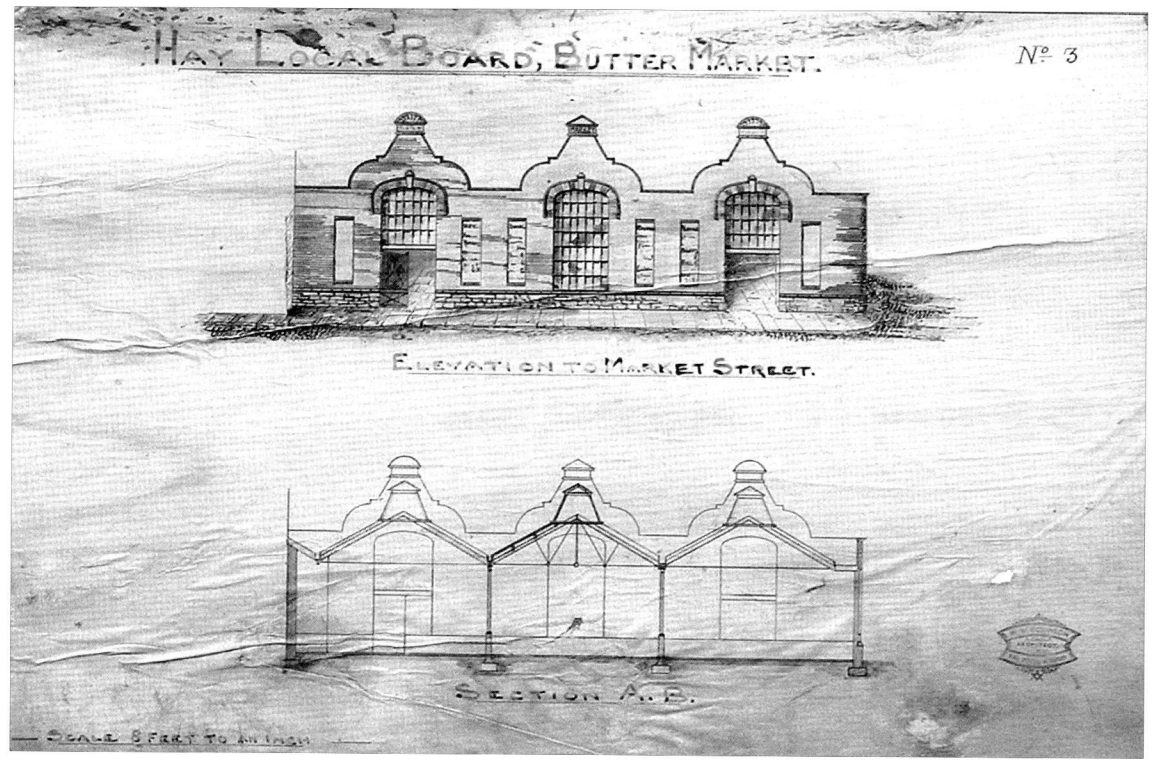

The elevation plan above gives some idea of the proposed appearance of the hall.

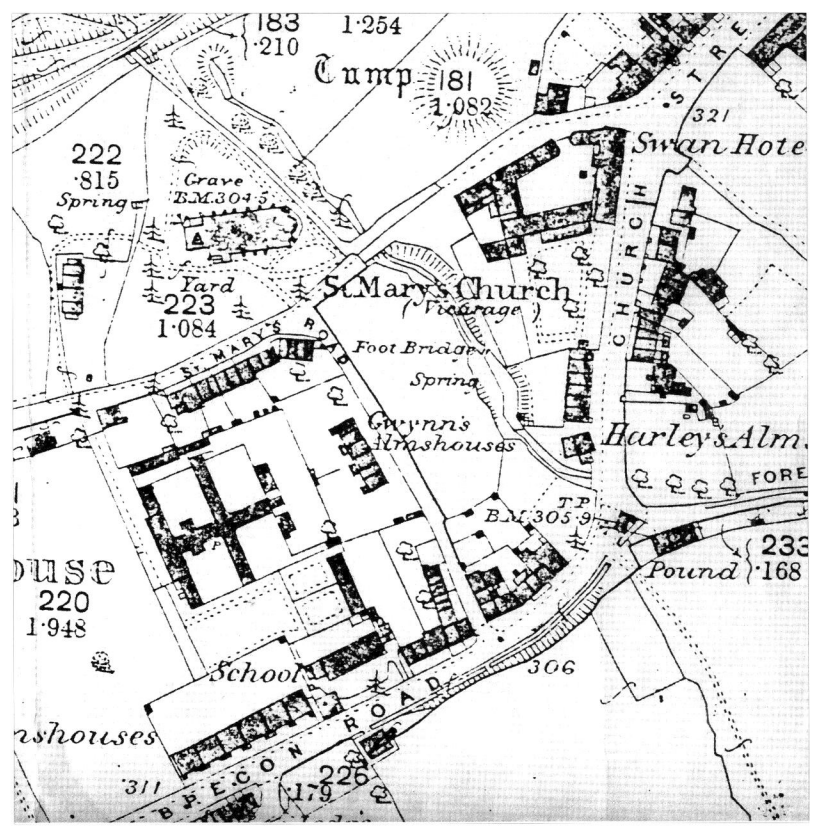

A section of an O.S. plan dated 1885. It is unusual because it shows the position of the toll house at the bottom of Church Street with the junction of Brecon Road and Forest Road.

This must have been the toll gate people tried to avoid by using Gipsy Castle Lane. This led to the building of the double road leading to Hay Church.
(See page 6, chapter 2.)

Map courtesy Ordnance Survey Office.

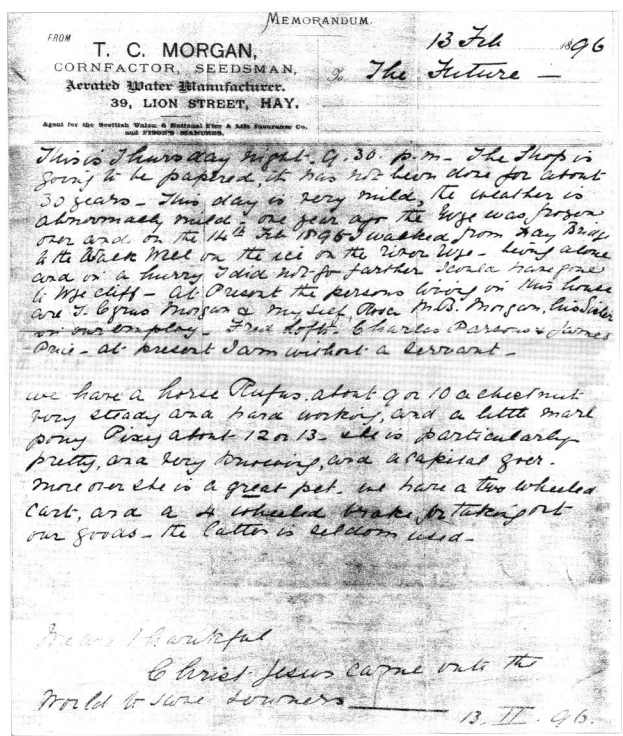

13th February 1896
To   THE FUTURE

This is Thursday night - 9.30 p.m. The shop is going to be papered, it has not been done for about 30 years. This day is very mild, the weather is abnormally mild. One year ago the Wye was frozen over and on the 14th February 1895 I walked from Hay Bridge to the Walk Mill on the ice on the River Wye. Being alone and in a hurry I did not go farther I could have gone to Wye Cliff. At present the persons living in this house are T. Cyrus Morgan and myself, Rosa M.B. Morgan, his sister. In our employ Fred Lofts - Charles Parsons and James Price. At present I am without a servant. We have a horse Rufus, about 9 or 10 a chestnut, very steady and hard working, and a little mare pony Pixy about 12 or 13. She is particularly pretty, and very knowing, and a capital goer, moreover she is a great pet. We have a two wheeled cart, and a 4 wheeled brake for taking out our goods. The latter is seldom used.
We are thankful,
Christ Jesus came into the world to save sinners.
13.II.96

Copy of a letter found in an envelope marked "To the future" found in a wall in 1986 during renovation work at the building on the corner of Lion Street and Brook Street, now "Addyman's Books". A modern typed copy is shown alongside.
According to the 1881 census returns for Hay, Rosa was 43 years of age at the time of writing this letter. Her brother Thomas Cyrus, in 1881 was listed as a maltster. By 1896 they had improved their status in life as the letter heading above states that their business was 'corn factor, seedsman and aerated water manufacturer'.

TOWN HALL, HAY.

By Permission of the Worshipful the Mayor.

MR. WILLIAM WALTON DUNANT,

IN respectfully announcing to the Nobility, Gentry, and Inhabitants generally of HAY, and the surrounding Neighbourhood, that he intends opening the Theatre on SATURDAY the 16th. of January, 1841, begs to ask their patronage and support, having engaged a respectable and talented Company, and being fully resolved to spare neither study nor exertion in bringing before the public a series of novel and intellectual amusements, in such a style as to merit that support which he now most respectfully solicits.

Mr. Dunant has had the honour to be patronized by the following distinguished families:—The Right Hon. Earl of Powis, Countess of Lisburne, Lady Hudart, Miss Agusta Wynne, Mrs. Powell, the Rev. Dean of Bangor, Sir R. Buckley, Bart. M. P. R. H. Fazakerla, Esq. D. Bertham, Esq. General Manners Kerr, Lloyd of Ragget, Esq. R. W. Price, Esq. Rhiwlas, Lord Willowby, De Eresby, W. Little, Esq Nanney, Esq. Belmont, R. Read, Esq. Mr. Evans, George Mears, Esq. David Evans, Esq. N. Matthew, Esq. Col. Powell, Captain Powel, Colonel Sir J. Edwards, Bart, M. P. C. D. Humphreys, Esq. Dr. Southam, W. Lloyd, Esq. W. W. C. Wynne, Esq. R. Richards, Esq. M. P. Caerynwch, H. Richards, Esq. Dr. Tudor, Sir B. and Lady Hall, Mrs. Hanbury Williams, Captain Egerton, J. Bailie, Esq. M. P. Ditto Jun. M. P. &c. &c.

BY DESIRE,
AND
UNDER THE PATRONAGE OF
COL. POWELL,
OF THE HARDWICKE.

On SATURDAY Evening, JANUARY 16, 1841,
Will be performed an admired Piece, (never acted here) Called—A

LOAN OF A LOVER.

Old Swivel	MR. ROWLANDS.	Delve	MR. THORNHILL.
Peter Spike	MR. DUNANT.	Capt. Arnstoff	Mr. WELLUM.
Gertrude, with Songs,	MRS. WELLUM.	Ernistine	MRS. DUNANT.

END OF THE PLAY.
DANCE, BY MR. ROWLANDS.

AFTER WHICH, THE ADMIRED PIECE OF—THE

Day After THE WEDDING.

	Colonel Freelove	MR. WELLUM.	
Lord Rivers ... MR. THORNHILL.	James ... MR. DUNANT.	Groom ... MR. ROWLANDS.
Lady Freelove ... Mrs. WELLUM,	Mrs. Davies ... MRS. DUNANT.	

END OF THE INTERLUDE.
FAVORITE SINGING, BY MRS. WELLUM.
Comic Song, by Mr. Dunant.

The whole to conclude with the new and admired farce, called

BACHELOR'S BUTTONS.

In which MRS. DUNANT will sustain FOUR different Characters.

Old Wilton	MR. ROWLANDS.	Harry Thornton	MR. THORNHILL.
Sam	MR. DUNANT.		
Maria			Mrs. DUNANT.

There is not, perhaps, within the whole range of social amusements one more worthy of our intellectual powers than this, and certainly none more replete with greater variety or endued with more fascinating charms. The theatre is the temple of arts, and in no place is their influence more deeply felt. All civilised communities have invariably been anxious to promote the welfare of their national theatres; and precisely at those periods, when refinement has been carried to the highest pitch, has this solicitude most generally prevailed. At the very origin of its institution, the sages of Greece were foremost among the promoters of theatricals; and, with very few exceptions, the greatest and wisest men of all countries have from that time to the present been its patrons. And surely, none but those who would deny as amusements of every kind and indiscriminately denounce all enjoyments (however lawful and innocent) could prohibit a recreation like this, which gives so wide a scope for the exercise and display of the highest faculties of the mind, and which, at the same time, presents so rich a combination of intellectual delight.

Door open at Half-past Six; to commence at Seven.
Pit, 2s.—Gallery, 1s.—Back Seats, 6d.—Children half-price. Tickets to be had at the Printer's.

W. HARRIS, PRINTER, HAY.

A poster printed by W. Harris of Hay announcing that a travelling band of thespians would be coming to Hay on Saturday 16th January 1841.

They were to appear at "the Town Hall" which is believed to be situated where the Cheese Market now stands at the end of Market Street.

The 'flowery' language used in this early Victorian poster is typical of advertisements from this period and the century before.

The charges for admission seem to be quite expensive as the "Pit was 2s., Gallery 1s., Back seats 6d. - Children half price".

A poster printed by H. R. Grant advertising the proposed celebrations for peace after World War I in Hay.

The dance was held at the Agricultural Hall in Lion Street which is now Richard Booth's main bookshop. From contemporary accounts it was all a huge success and the dance event was full to overflowing.

One amusing point in the poster is where it states that 'Peace Mugs will be presented to all children.....'. Someone has pencilled in between 'peace mugs' and 'will' the words "if received in time".

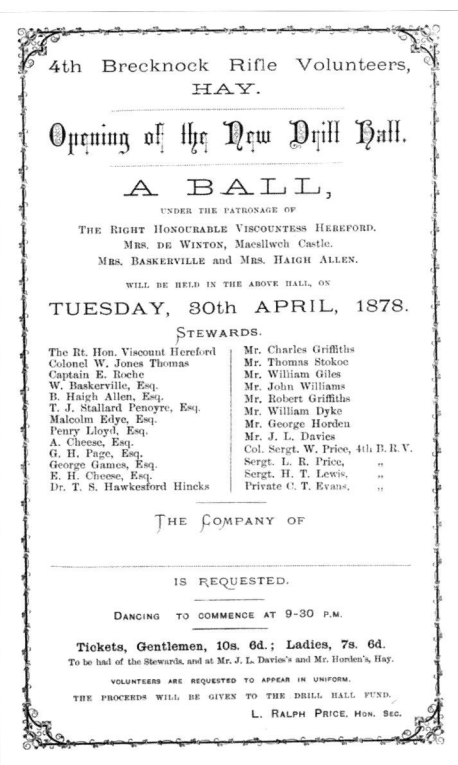

The frontispiece of the invitation leaflet for the opening of the Drill Hall in Lion Street on Tuesday, 30th April 1878.

The building was used until the 1980s by army authorities. It has now been refurbished as an art gallery.

HAY & CUSOP PEACE CELEBRATIONS,
JULY 19th, 1919.

All Sailors and Soldiers are cordially invited to take part in the following festivities which have been arranged under the auspices of Hay and Cusop Sailors and Soldiers Reception Committee.

Programme of Events.

11.0 a.m. MEET at HAY TOWN CLOCK.

11.15 **PROCESSION** headed by the TOWN BAND and members of Hay and Cusop Councils, to proceed to the Parish Church for UNITED THANKSGIVING SERVICE.
(Marshal: Mr. E. G. Mayall)

12.30 p.m. Invitation **DINNER & RECEPTION** to all returned Soldiers and Sailors residing in, or visiting, Hay or Cusop.
Other gentlemen desirous of attending the dinner to assist in welcoming our gallant men should apply to the Secretaries for tickets (4/6 each) on or before Friday, July 18th.
The Dinner will be presided over by Councillor F. Cadman, Chairman of the Hay U.D.C., assisted by Mr. C. E. Tunnard Moore, Chairman of the Cusop Parish Council.

3.0 **SPORTS** on "The Warren," by kind permission of Mr. F. Goodwin. For particulars see small bills. Children's Sports will be arranged for on the ground.

4.30 to 6.30 **FREE TEA** to all residents of HAY and CUSOP. All School Children must bring their own cups.

7 to 8.30 **CARNIVAL** to start from Hay Station. For Prizes and further particulars, see handbills.

9 to 10.30. Ascents at the Town Clock of Fire Balloons and Rockets.

9 to 12. **DANCE** at the Agricultural Hall, to which all returned Soldiers and Sailors with a lady companion are heartily invited. Refreshments free.
A charge 2/6 each will be made for all others wishing to attend. Refreshments free. Tickets may be obtained from the Hon. Secs. and from Mr. H. R. Grant, Stationer, Hay.

PEACE MUGS *(if received in time)* will be presented to all Children on the School Registers of the Hay and Cusop Schools at the close of afternoon school, on Friday, July 18th.

Parents of Children under school age may obtain the Presentation Mugs for their Children by applying at the Schools immediately after the distribution to the School Children.

H. MORRIS,
H. GILBY, } Hon. Secs.

Hay, July 10th.

H. R. Grant, Printer and Stationer, Castle Street, Hay.

A patriotic calendar issued by Gwatkin, the grocer in Lion Street, for the year 1915. It shows H.M. King George V together with prominent military characters and politicians of the day.

The shop then became Evans' grocery stores and is now the Chinese 'take away' restaurant.

south view of The Hay, Brecknock

A unique pencil drawing of Hay by an unknown artist. The date is uncertain but seems to be from the early part of the nineteenth century.
Print courtesy Mrs. J. A. Hutchins

The programme of the celebrations in Hay for the coronation of Queen Elizabeth II in 1953.

The programme contains many contemporary advertisements for local shops and companies. The proposed events were considerable and consisted of civic parades, variety shows, a coronation ball, children's sports, socials and carnivals.

BEAUTYFUL HAY.

WELSH HAY, let me thy praises sing,
　Before my pleasant thoughts take wing,
Thy frowning mountains, winding Wye,
Instruct the mind and please the eye.

The mountains take you back in thought,
To when Creation's work was wrought,
And as the distance back you scan,
You truly say, how weak is man.

The river in its silent glide,
Sweeps on to meet the ocean tide,
Drawn up in clouds again to fall,
Emblem of Eternity to all.

Stroll slowly down the banks of Wye,
Look out o'er stream for Jock Scot fly.
'Tis pleasant then, in evening cool,
To see the salmon leap the pool.

Monster fish of course are killed,
The Angler's creel is always filled;
Big trout are caught and by-the-bye,
Fishermen never tell a lie.

Our Hills are a constant lure,
Attacks of nerves they always cure;
Leave the office and the shop,
Enjoy the breeze from mountain top.

"Is life worth living?" "Yes," I say,
"Just come and stay in healthy Hay,
It's mountain air, Wye's winding stream,
A paradise beyond a dream."

　　　　　　　　　　W. WALLIS.

A poem about 'Beautiful Hay' written by W. Wallis in the 1930s and turned into a postcard.

The frontispiece of the programme for the ceremony of opening the new bridge over the river Wye on 14th January 1958.

OLD STREET NAMES

These are some of the street names mentioned in census returns and documents before 1877. Their new name and probable location are shown.

Tramroad	Wyeford Road
Ship Street	Top of Newport Street
Tabernacle Walk	?
Coal Wharf	The present cattle market
Church Yard	?
Back Lane	Belmont Road
Mill Street	Part of Heol-y-Dwr nearest Broad Street
Pig Lane	Lower (nearest Broad Street) Chancery Lane
Gravel Lane	Top Chancery Lane (behind Wheat Sheaf)
Red Lion Street	Town Clock end of Lion Street
Black Lion Street	Top Heol-y-Dwr to Black Lion
High Street	High Town
Horsefair Road	Oxford Road
Taverntrap	Possibly Back Fold
Prospect Terrace	?
Prospect Place	?
Royal Oak Row	Brecon Road (from Cemetery Lane running west)
Dishpool Lane	Forest Road
Cardigan Hall	Top Cemetery Lane
Buttermarket Street	Market Street
Cranbourne Alley	The Pavement
George Street	Church Street
Half Moon Street	Part of Lion Street by Parish Hall
Chain Alley	Bottom of Newport Street (demolished c.1880)
Leatherbottle Street	Part of Heol-y-Dwr

INDEX OF CONTENTS

Aden - Territorial Army - Hay Division	88	Cater's shop on The Pavement	24
Aerial view of Hay by Wilson	41	Cats Park in Newport Street	34
Albion Terrace - building of	52	Cattle sale in Broad Street	32
Aldershot 1892 Hay Volunteers	85	Chain Alley	34
Archdeacon Bevan at the gate of Hay Castle	3	Chancery Lane in 1963	35
Archery group	71	China Market in Market Street	37
Armstrong, Herbert Rowse - reference to	80	Choir - Hay male voice	52
"At the Hay" print of 1814	26	Church Lads' Brigade	82
Bailey Walk	38	Church parade in Church Street	51
Band outside Drill Hall	85	Church tower - view from	33
Baptist Sunday School	10	Concert at Town Hall - poster 1841	94
Barrett, headmaster outside school in Brecon Road	67	Congregational Sunday School	10
Barrett, headmaster portrait	80	Conservative Club - builders outside	55
Bell Bank - new fire engine	65	Coronation 1953 - brochure	97
Bevan, Archdeacon jubilee celebrations	50	Coronation display - George V in Castle Street	51
Bevan, Bishop of Swansea and Brecon - portrait	78	Council school in 1910	68
Black Lion Inn	43	Council school in 1916	69
Blue Boar Inn	19	Council school pupils in 1930	69
Bon Marché in Castle Square	21	Council school pupils in 1939	70
Bottling factory demolition	21	Council school pupils on nature walk 1948	70
Bottling factory in High Town	21	Cycle club	73
Brecon Road flood in 1930	54	Darnley's print of Hay Castle	2
Brecon Road stores	36	Davies, chemist shop	48
Brickworks railway on Cusop Hill	40	De Winton - vicar with Ford car	55
Bridge - new, opening leaflet 1957	97	Demolition of Hay railway station 1963	63
Bridge - original stone structure	11	Demolition of Chancery Lane houses	35
Bridge Street view in 1890	42	De Winton - vicar with Ford car	55
Bridge, new, opening ceremony	14	Display at Warren - fire brigade	64
Bridge, new, work in progress	13	Drill Hall - opening invitation	95
Broad Street in 1901	32	Empire Day flag at Church school	67
Broad Street in 1912	31	Evans CT and firemen display of	66
Broad Street in 1920	31	Firefly - for breaking up	66
Bryne's shop in Bear Street	49	Firefly in Broad Street	65
Buffaloes, Order of - group at Crown	83	Flag ceremony at Town Clock	26
Butcher's shop at St. John's Chapel	8	Floods at Dulais Terrace	56
Butcher's shop in Lion Street	46	Football team 1923	74
Cadman's shop in Broad Street	42	Football team 1925	73
Cae Mawr - view from Castle	39	Football team 1933-34 season	76
Calendar - Gwatkin advert	96	Football team 1951	76
Camp of RHA at New Forest Farm	87	Football team outside Parish Hall	72
Card players	73	Football team, winners at Hereford	75
Carnival - W.I. members	77	Footbridge, railway - view from 1920	59
Carnival 1953	77	Footbridge, railway - view looking east	62
Castle - print from 1830	1	Footbridge, railway - view looking west	62
Castle as it is now	4	Foresters' meeting at Town Clock	28
Castle from the south	4	Foundation stone - laying of at Hay Church	89
Castle from the top of Hay Town Clock	4	Games, John	78
Castle Square - plan of 1868	91	Gas workers in Church Street	48
Castle Square and High Town 1870	20	Giles ironmongers - advert	45
Castle Square and High Town 2002	20	Golf Club members	75
Castle staff postcard of 1915	3	Guardians, Board of	81
Castle Street in 1870	15	Gwatkin's shop in Lion Street	48
Castle Street in 1914	18	Gwilliam's shop in High Town	46
Castle Street in 1930	17	Half Moon in Lion Street	46
Castle Street in 1949	17	Harding, Rhys - playing organ	82
Castle Street in 1959	17	Hay, stone lithograph of, from the north	58

High Town from St. John's Place 1900	23
High Town from St. John's Place 1925	23
Hockey team	72
Home Guard - Hay and District	88
Horden's shop in Castle Street	15
Horse fair in Oxford Road	33
Howells, Albert, town crier	84
Hunt meeting at Castle	72
Jones, Percival, Senator	78
Jones, Ralph, presentation to	10
Kedward's shop in Broad Street	31
Letter found in wall - Lion Street	93
Lewis the butcher at St. John's Chapel	7
Lilwall slide of High Town	22
Lilwall slide of High Town and Giles, ironmongers	22
Madigan's shop and car	18
Market day 1930	30
Market day at Town Clock 1920	30
Market day in Broad Street	32
Market Hall - elevation view	92
Market Hall - proposed new - plan of	92
Marwood Rev. at Congregational Chapel	10
Mikado - performance of at Drill Hall	74
Mill at Cusop	39
Moor house	34
Morris, Harry - school group	67
Morris, Harry - portrait of	80
Motte & Bailey - artist's impression	1
Moxon, Thomas, wedding of	79
Moxon's advert	16
NFS firemen in 1941	66
Notice of charges - fire	64
Old street names	98
Oxford Road - fire brigade 1923	65
Oxford Road looking east	35
Parade in Church Street	19
Parish Hall school	68
Peace celebrations 1919 - poster advertising	95
Pencil drawing of Hay	96
Poem on postcard about Hay	97
Post box by the Town Clock	30
Post Office - Radnor House	44
Pram in Castle Street	19
Pugh, T. A. fruiterer in Lion Street	49
Pugh, William, fireman uniform	64
Pugh's shop on The Pavement	24
Punt on river - view by Moxon	40
Repairs to town clock in 1923	28
River view by Moxon	40
Robert Williams - staff outside	45
Robert Williams Ltd - advert for	45
Royal Horse Artillery - the blacksmith	87
Royal Horse Artillery at canteen	87
Royal Horse Artillery at New Forest	86
Royal Horse Artillery with field gun	87
"Salt Box" houses in Oxford Road	44
Savin's cast iron bridge	11
Ship Inn from Newport Street	43
Shop on The Pavement	24
Show - Hay - Webb's display	54
Signal box - view inside	61
Smith, Ken, town crier	84
Snow in 1983	25
Spike Island	79
St. John's Ambulance Brigade at Town Clock	81
St. John's Chapel as a barber's shop	7
St Mary's Church - the toll gate	6
St. Mary's Church - print by Henry Gastineau	5
St. Mary's Church - the toll road approach	6
Station - view of looking east	61
Station - view towards town from down platform	61
Stokoe - air trip	54
Storm at Hay - report of	89
Sunday School parade outside George House	51
Sundial at cemetery	37
Swan Bank in 1900	33
Swan Well	36
Telephone exchange, closing	57
Tennis at Liberal Club	74
Terrett's shop in Broad Street	28
Three Tuns, repairs	42
Timber on carriages at Town Clock	29
Timber yard - Robt. Williams Ltd.	49
Tinto House, Broad Street	31
Toll gates opening of, Hay Bridge	12
Toll house on Bridge Street	41
Town Clock from The Pavement	25
Town Council members 1960	83
Train arriving - 1950	62
Train from Brecon arriving	59
Train passing under Hay Bridge	60
Tramway - plan of 1814	90
Tramway - print of	58
Tree felling at The Moor	29
Tucker's shop in Castle Street	16
Tump - plan of from 1853	90
Volunteers at Hay	86
War Memorial in front of Hay Castle	4
War Memorial opening ceremony	53
Warren view by Moxon	36
Webbs - cycle shop in Lion Street	47
Webbs - hearses on display	47
Webbs - workshop in Church Street	47
Webbs - workshop interior	47
Webbs' staff outside works in Lion Street	52
Wesleyan chapel in Brecon Road	9
Williams, Billy, Lt. fire brigade uniform	64
Williams, butcher in Castle Street	18
Wilson, Doctor and wife	81
Women's Institute, Inauguration	57

The author and publishers are grateful to the following people who have subscribed to this book prior to publication.

The names are listed in alphabetical order and as requested on application form.

Bruce Addyman
Addyman - Brichto
Donald Addyman
Nick Angus
Mike Anthony
Mavis Anthony
Joan and Jeffery Babb
Michael and Jeannette Barker
Caroline Beagley
Roger and Dawn Beetham
Nigel Birch
Julian and Diana Blunt
Tony and Diane Bray
Christiana and Kevin Brook
The Brookfield House Archive
Alison Brown
Francis P. Burke
Debra (Debs) Byers
Susan Campbell
Edmund Carlisle
David Cash
June & Leonard Chase
Frank and Geraldine Cleary
Annette Cobbold
Frances Copping
David Crane
Garry and Ann Cruea
Anne M. J. Cuthbertson
Arwyn and Lavinia Davies
Christopher P. Davies
Mrs. Teddy Davies
Kevin and Debbie Davies & family
Mary Esther Davies
Ann and Frank Davies
Colin and Cynthia Davies
Diana Davies
Steve and Zena Davies
Carol and Will Davies
Sheila A. Duggan
Emma Dunn
David Dunn
Paul Elkington
Edgar and Iris Evans
John Evans
Gwyneth Elizabeth Price Evans
Huw David Evans
James Derek Evans
Mark Evans
Richard Charles Evans
Dawn Farnworth
Joan Ferguson

Neal Field
James Derek Evans
Elizabeth Fry
Paul Gerrish
Christopher Gibbons
Andrew Gibson-Watt
Reginald Gilbert
Jan Golding
Mary & Robert Golesworthy
Roger and Anna Golesworthy
Eleri Golesworthy
Annie and Ian Goold
Brian A. Gorringe M.B.E.
Gretta Gover
Martin Grafton
Eddie Grafton
Joan and Frank Green
Nicola J. Green
Jeremy Griffin
Ifor G. Griffiths
David and Ann Grosvenor
Peter Harries
Brian and Heather Harris
Albert Haver
Rosie Hayles
Peter and Annie Howard
Steven and Prue Howells
Peter Howells
Michael Howells
Christopher Hughes
Jim Hyatt
Ken Jenkins
Barbara Jenkins
Ishy and Betty Jones
David and Carolyn Jones
Bette Jones
David Owen Price Jones
Daisy I. L. Jones
Howell Walter Price Jones
Luther Jones
Ivor and Ann Jones
Laurence Middleton Jones
Richard Gethin-Jones
Roderick Edward Jones
James Kemp-Slaughter
Clive and Cherry Keylock
Nigel Keylock
Robert J. Knights
Mr. J. F. P. Lally
Sue and Gordon Lawrence
Sheila Leighton & family

Jean Letts
Anne Lewis
Reg and Nesta Lewis
John Lewis
Peter and Rita Like
Lynda Like
Janet and Brynmor Like
Martin Like & family
Mrs. F. Lloyd née Evans
Hilda Lockwood
Mac and Nina Maddy
Gloria Mary Madigan
Michael Thomas Madigan
Peter James Mathers
Sylvia Mayall
Rosemary Montague
Leon Morelli
Julia Morelli
David C. Morgan
Reg and Mona Morgan
Tony and Meriel Morgan
Nigel and Rilla Morries
John Morris
Garfield James Morris
Diane Nicholls
Denys Parry
Stephen Parry
Mrs. Mary Penoyre Morgan
Malcolm Perry
Roger Perry
Wyndham Powell
Robert J. Powell
Ted Powell
Lee Donat Price
Denys Alec Price
David George Patrick Price
David Harry Price
John and Margaret Price
Trevor P. Price
Stuart Pritchard
Alan Powell
Louise Probert
Caroline Pryce-Mason
Vera Pryce-Mason
Anthony H. Pugh
Ethel Pugh
John Pugh
Raymond and Sylvia Pugh
Tim and Sarah Pugh
Samuel Pugh
Thomas Pugh
Julian and Gillian Raffell
Teresa and Stephen Ratcliffe
John Reese
Peter and Olwen Roberts

Mark and Janet Robinson
Mrs. Mary Ruff
Stephen Salter
Betty and Karl Showler
Julysia Sinclair
Adam Sinclair
June Smith
Deborah E. M. Smith
Gillian and Ken Smith
Barbara and Derek Smith
William and Pauline Smith
Malcolm and Shirley Smith
Angela Karen Smith
Mrs. J. O. Smith née Price
Michael Smith
Hugh Oliver Spankie
Richard J. Stevenson
Peter and Maureen Sutton
Gwyneth and Frank Taylor
John and Mary Thomas
Sian Elisabeth Thomas
Margaret W. Thompson
Jackie and David Uren
Mel Walford
Philip Watkins
Winifred Constance Webb
Mrs. E.A.Webb
Adrian Webb
Betty Weir and Vera North
Sarah Jane Wigington
Bryan Wigington
Richard and Mandy Wildee
Sid Wilding
Brian Wilding
Gwyneth Williams
Hazel Williams
James and Rose Marie Williams
Jenny and David Williams
John Godfrey Williams
R. R. Williams